# THE JIM THORPE STORY

Once in a lifetime a star is born and it shines with such brillance that nothing can transcend it. Such a star was Jim Thorpe, greatest football star and all-around athlete of this century, who continued to play professional ball beyond the age of most men. In a recent sport poll he was again named All Star-All American. Great athletes come and go, but no one has yet topped Thorpe's records for football, baseball, field and track.

# THE
# JIM THORPE
## STORY

### *America's Greatest Athlete*

by

GENE SCHOOR

with

HENRY GILFOND

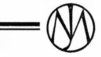

JULIAN MESSNER     NEW YORK

Published simultaneously in the United States and Canada by
Julian Messner, a division of Simon & Schuster, Inc.,
1 West 39 Street, New York, N.Y. 10018. All rights reserved.

Eighteenth Printing, 1972

Printed in the United States of America
ISBN 0-671-32525-6 MCE

*I*KE EISENHOWER sat on the Army bench, his eyes glued on that great Indian who was slashing and smashing away at the West Point line, tearing it to shreds. The ball swished back from center and "that Indian" had it again. He moved in quick, short strides behind his interference and there he was again out in the open, his knees shooting up and down to his chin like well-oiled pistons. Ike clenched his strong jaws. It was another first down for little Carlisle, the Indian school, and "that Indian" with the pugnacious Irish chin was treating the whole Army eleven as if it were a sieve, just full of holes.

West Point was on the verge of a humiliating defeat. Cadet Eisenhower shifted restlessly on the bench. He twisted his football helmet in his hands. If Army was to do anything on the gridiron that afternoon, "that Indian" would have to be stopped. And there was only one way to stop him. Get him out of the line-up. Put him back on the bench. Knock him out!

The coach gave Ike the nod. Eisenhower, tabbed

All-American by a host of eastern sports writers, eagerly got up on his feet, trotted out on the playing field,
every muscle in his body flexed to the purpose to which
he had set himself. He tapped the left halfback he was
replacing.

"I'll get that man if it's the last thing I do," he said.

The back smiled at Eisenhower but Ike didn't see it.
He was wrapped up in the huddle.

"That Indian," he said, turning to the right halfback.
"Next time he comes through, let's give him the high-
low."

There was no mistaking which Indian he meant.
There were eleven Indians West Point faced that afternoon back in 1912, but there was one who was a team
in himself. And Ike knew that if "that Indian" carried
the ball there was no question about whether he would
bull his way through the line into the secondaries. He
had been coming through tackle, through guard,
through center, as if they weren't there at all.

"I'll get the Indian high," said Ike. "You get him
low."

If the high-low worked, the two Army backs knew,
"that Indian" wasn't going to be of much more use to
his team for the rest of that football game anyway.
One of the backs would tackle him high on one side,
near the shoulder line. The other would tackle him
low, about the knees or lower. If the play was timed
properly, they could almost break the man in two.
The two West Pointers didn't want to kill the Indian.

But they were two great competitors with a will to win. They wanted to win that game from the highly publicized and highly vaunted Carlisle.

The Indian school had the ball. Army knew that the man who would carry it was the man they needed to stop for good. The two Army backs primed themselves. They tensed as the Carlisle quarterback snapped off the signals.

"84 . . . 96 . . . 33 . . ."

The ball shot back from center. Line hit line. "That Indian" was carrying the pigskin. The two West Pointers poised. They hit that man with the ball. They hit him as they had planned to hit him. It was the one-two and the Indian was stopped.

"He gained ground. He always gained ground," Ike Eisenhower will tell you. He remembers the day and the game with awe and with reverence. "He was the greatest football man I've ever seen," he'll remark with a respectful wag of his head. "But that one-two really stopped him."

When the two cadets got up from the gridiron the Indian was stretched out flat on the ground. For a moment or two he didn't move at all and for a minute or two West Point thought that the stretchers would have to come out on the field. Then the Indian blinked his eyes, pulled himself up to his feet and staggered back into the Carlisle line.

"We figured he was through for the day," says Ike Eisenhower. "We were pretty sure that he wasn't going to run any more plays. We were certain that he wasn't going to gain another yard for that Carlisle team the rest of that afternoon for sure."

The Army boys set themselves for the next play with a little more confidence. Whoever was going to carry the ball for the Indian team, it wasn't going to be that man that West Point hadn't been able to stop. That was the way they saw it as the Carlisle quarterback began to call numbers again.

"42 . . . 87 . . . 26. . . ."

The center snapped the ball into the backfield. The backfield went into motion. And the man with the pigskin was . . . "that Indian" again. And right through the Army line he went, as if it were made up of seven tin soldiers. And into the secondaries he plunged, ten yards, before he was brought down.

"First down for Carlisle!"

All afternoon he moved up and down that gridiron as if he owned it.

Army kicked off. The Indian caught the ball on his own ten-yard line. He picked up his interference. He was up to the twenty-, the thirty-, the forty-yard line. He passed the fifty-yard mark and he shot out from behind his own men. He was in the clear. There was no stopping him. Straight down the field he ran, swift as a deer, till he passed the last chalk mark and looked out to the referee to raise his hand to signify another touchdown for Carlisle.

But the whistle had blown. Carlisle had been offside.

THE JIM THORPE STORY

Army breathed a sigh of relief and took the ball out of the Indian's hands.

They kicked off again. This time the Indian picked up the pigskin on his five-yard line. Again the interference. And again the yards were peeled off under his fast feet. Again he pushed out from his own interference and again he was in the clear. This time the referee's hand went up.

"I guess that was the longest run for a touchdown I ever made," the Indian will tell his listeners. "Ninety and ninety-five make one hundred eighty-five yards."

He was phenomenal. Deceptive, fast, leaving his would-be tacklers and his tacklers dazed on the field, he ran the highly touted Army team and its All-American candidates ragged.

When the final whistle blew to end the festivities the score was 27-6 and it was Carlisle that carted off the goal posts. The Indian? He played the full sixty minutes of the savage, clean, but hard-hitting game, without a substitute for a single play. Ike Eisenhower? He limped off the field with a painfully twisted knee which eventually was to cut short his football career.

Ike, of course, was our own five-star general, David Dwight "Ike" Eisenhower, the man who as supreme commander of the Allied Forces in Europe, beat Hitler's armies into unconditional surrender, and who is now Supreme Commander of the United Nations in western Europe.

"That Indian" was the greatest athlete America has

ever produced in its great history in the field of sports. His name is Wa-Tho-Huck. Translated from the language of the Sac and Fox Indians, the name means Bright Path. It was indeed a bright path in almost every possible athletic venture that the great Indian blazed for himself and for the glory of his country. You know him better—everybody in the world who is in the least interested in athletics knows him better—by that simple name, Jim Thorpe.

"I am not, as many believe," says Jim Thorpe, "a full-blooded Indian. I am five-eights Indian; three-eighths Potawatomie on my mother's side and two-eighths Sac and Fox on my father's side."

But when a ten pound baby came to that one-room log cabin on the North Canadian River, just outside the Indian reservation, Charlotte View Thorpe knew that her newborn son had inherited all the valiant qualities of her heroic grandfather, the great Sac and Fox chief, Black Hawk. She looked out of the window. The sun was shining brightly and it lit up the path leading to her cabin. It was then that she named her boy Wa-Tho-Huck, Bright Path. He was christened James Francis Thorpe. Jimmy was one of two boys. His brother was named Charles. Charles was the dark, copper-colored Indian. James was all Indian, too, but he was lighter in color and he had that strong, stubborn Irish jaw. It was James who inherited the greatest traits, the prowess, the strength, the fighting heart of his great ancestors.

Chief Black Hawk, Jim Thorpe's great-grandfather, was a powerful man. He was strong and fast on his feet. When he was still a young brave he won the respect and admiration of his people as the best runner, the best jumper, the best wrestler and the best swimmer of the tribe. This was the tribe of the Sac and Fox. Many many years before, the Sac Indians and the Fox Indians had been two separate peoples. They met somewhere near Green Bay in Wisconsin and joined forces to become a more powerful and dangerous tribe. Black Hawk became one of their greatest chiefs. He was only fifteen years old when he gained recognition from the older braves of the Fox and the Sac for his bravery in battle. At seventeen he was intrusted with his first serious mission and led a war party against the mighty Osage Indians, a rival tribe. It was in this foray that Black Hawk took his first scalp. Two years later, when he was no more than nineteen, he led two hundred of his people in a fight against two hundred Cherokee Indians and covered himself with glory. Fully half of the Cherokee were left dead on the field of battle that day. He fought the white man, too. But the white man was destined to conquer. Step by step the Indians who opposed the coming of the paleface were pushed back. The Indians were no match for the arms and strength of the white people. But even in his last stand Black Hawk was majestic.

"The sun rose dim on us in the morning," said the Sac and the Fox chieftain, "and at night it sank in a dark cloud and looked like a ball of fire. My sun is setting and will rise no more."

There was humility in Black Hawk but there was also great pride. No champion ever hung up his boxing gloves, no athlete ever bade farewell to his spiked shoes, with greater dignity. Black Hawk had fought his last battle. He bowed down to the superior strength of the younger and more vigorous white people who had moved into his land. The year was 1832. He retired to the Indian reservation, set up near Fort Des Moines, where he spent his last years in peace.

"All the world loves a lover, a fighter and an athlete," Jim Thorpe has said. "My great-grandfather, Black Hawk, was all of these."

Jim Thorpe's great career in sports has never been equaled in the memory of man, never been approached by any other single athlete. And Jim Thorpe says, "I am no more proud of my career as an athlete than I am of the fact that I am a direct descendant of that noble warrior."

It was in the 1830's that an Irishman by the name of Thorpe came to live among the Indians settled near Fort Des Moines, taking as his wife a young Indian girl. The Indian girl was a granddaughter of the great warrior, Chief Black Hawk. To this union there came a son. The son was named Hiram Thorpe.

Hiram was half Irish but he was a true descendant of the Sac and the Fox brave who had been their last leader. Not only did he look almost completely Indian, but he strongly resembled his grandfather, Black Hawk, and the resemblance was not just a matter of skin, color of hair and shape of nose. Hiram Thorpe was physically a powerful man. He was over six feet tall and weighed two hundred and thirty pounds. Like his chieftain grandfather, he was such a tower of strength that very few of the young Indians on the reservation were willing to compete with him in any physical sport. Like his grandfather before him, Hiram loved his freedom and would not surrender it without a struggle. When the white men who governed the Indian reservation in the name of the White Father in Washington, D. C., began to make new rules for the red men, rules which cut into the rights of the Indians, Hiram Thorpe moved away from Fort Des Moines. With a number of companions he headed for the Indian territory in Oklahoma.

In Oklahoma Hiram Thorpe married for a second time. His first wife had died at Fort Des Moines. Their two children had been left in the school on the reservation. The second wife was Charlotte View. Charlotte was three-fourths Sac and Fox and one-fourth French. It was Charlotte View Fox who gave birth to Wa-Tho-Huck, Bright Path, James Francis Thorpe and his twin brother Charles.

The family was living in a crude cabin three miles south of Bellemont. You might have difficulty in locating it even on a big map. You might have better luck if you tried to find Shawnee, just a few miles north of Bellemont. The one-room cabin was actually on the banks of the North Canadian River, in the midst of a farming area about five miles from the Indian Territory line in Oklahoma. Hiram had claimed his one hundred and sixty acres per member of an Indian family, as the United States Government had decreed. It was here that the first child of his second union was born. They named him George. James Francis and his twin brother came seven years later on May 28, 1888. This was exactly one hundred years after Great-grandfather Black Hawk had been named chief of the Sac and the Fox. It was an auspicious celebration of a memorable day in the life of a great man. It was with joy and a flush of pride that Charlotte View Thorpe recognized the remarkable resemblance between her grandfather chief and one of her baby boys—James Francis.

## two

*I*'LL BEAT YOU to the old hickory tree!''

"No you won't!"

"Ready."

The two Indian boys toed the mark.

"Set."

Their bodies tensed.

"Go!"

As quick as two young hares, pell-mell through the shrub and the tall grass they ran. Step for step and stride for stride, their sun-burnt bodies almost touching, they raced for the old hickory tree. Their very lives might have depended on it. Ten yards, twenty, thirty, forty and, suddenly, there was space between them. Not much but enough.

"I beat you, Charlie."

"Beat you back to the barn!"

"Try."

Up and down they raced, between the barn and the

old hickory tree. Sometimes it was only a foot, sometimes it was a yard, but it was always the same. Charlie came in second.

"All right," he said. "You're a good runner, Jimmy."

"I have to be a good runner, Charlie." Jimmy grinned. He loved his twin brother. "I have to be a good runner to beat you."

"I'll wrestle you. I can beat you wrestling."

He knew that he always came out second best, but Charlie never gave up trying.

Jimmy shook his head, the big grin still on his mouth. "No you can't," he said, quietly.

For a minute they crouched perfectly still, as only Indians can be still. Charlie's hands were in front of him, poised to reach out suddenly and grip his opponent where he would least expect it. Jimmy's hands rested on his thighs. Their eyes were glued on each other. Their bodies swayed, then their feet began to mark out a circle. All at once they were at each other; arms and legs tangled, they fell to the ground with a dull thud, rolled, bumped, tumbled. Jimmy was on top, then Charlie, then Jimmy again. It was a rough, tough match between two boys who didn't know what it was to say, "Enough." The only sound that came from them as they strained every muscle in their bodies to win the fight was the heavy sound of their breathing. Only when he had Charlie's two shoulders firmly pinned to the earth did Jimmy speak.

"You're down!"

These were the Thorpe twins, Charles and James Francis. All day long they played together, racing, climbing, wrestling. They were inseparable during the first eight years of their lives. They roamed the prairies together, swam rivers, learned how to catch fish from the river with the spears of their ancestors'. There was nothing either one did that the other didn't do, too.

Of course there were other Indian boys on the reservation and also some white boys with whom the Thorpe twins played. Most of the games then were the games boys and girls play today. Their names might have been different. There was a game they played with darts. They called it misqua-pee. They also played fox and geese and another game they called deer and hound. The favorite game of the boys on the reservation, however, was "follow." Today it's called "follow the leader." Generally, however, it isn't as hard a game as the one the Thorpes played—and maybe it isn't as much fun.

"Many a time in these games," says Jim Thorpe, "I had to swim rivers, climb barns, jump off roofs, wade streams and ride horses."

Sometimes they would climb to the top of a tall tree that bent and swayed under their weight, then leap to the ground. Sometimes they had to run underneath a horse that got frisky with all the boys running under him.

It was a rough, tough game and you had to be rough and tough to play it. If you were caught "not following the leader," you had to go under the mill. The twenty or twenty-five boys playing the game would line up, spreading their legs, and the fellow who hadn't made the grade in the game would have to scamper on his hands and knees between all those legs. Of course he was helped by a good paddling, and those reservation boys could paddle!

The Thorpe twins played hard and grew strong and athletic. Then one day, when Jimmy and Charlie were eight, tragedy struck in the Thorpe home.

Charlie was ill. It was some form of pneumonia. The doctors didn't know as much then as they know today about pneumonia. They didn't have any of the wonderful life-saving drugs we now have. They didn't have sulfa or penicilin. They didn't have the iron lung. Charles Thorpe died when he was eight. Charlie and Jimmy were never going to wrestle again, never going to race for that old hickory tree again. It was a young but great companionship which had come to an abrupt end too soon.

Jim grew closer to his older brother George, after Charlie's death, and especially close to his father. He loved to watch big Hiram run, wrestle, swim, high jump and broad jump with the other menfolk who gathered in front of the Thorpe cabin after the day's work was done. Jim's father was a big man. No one could match him in any of the games the men played. He was champion wrestler, jumper, swimmer. Jim was pround of his father. He wanted to grow up to be a champion just like him.

When he was only six years old, young Jim would go along with his father on fishing and hunting trips. Charlie wanted to tag along but he wasn't as husky as his twin. He didn't have the stamina.

"Come along, Jim!" called Big Hiram, and out into the woods they would go, where the father taught the son how to trap bears and rabbits and raccoons. It was from Hiram that Jim learned to make steel traps and snares, how to make the figure-four trap out of corn stalks to trap quail. It was from Hiram that he learned how to ride a horse and how to shoot.

"Often," says Jim, "we would be gone for weeks."

Then they would pack their kill, mostly deer and bears, on the backs of their horses and start the long journey home by foot. Sometimes they would walk twenty and thirty miles a day.

"Once when we didn't have enough horses to carry our kill," recalls Jim, "my father slung a buck deer over each shoulder and carried them twenty miles to our home. I have never known a man with such energy. He could walk, ride and run for days without ever showing the least sign of fatigue."

It was when he was ten years old that Jim Thorpe used a gun for the first time. He was on one of the long hunting trips wtih his father. They had stopped along the side of a deer run. For a long time they crouched behind some bushes, neither father nor son breaking the silence. It may have been only minutes. Even to the calm, steady, patient young Jim, it seemed like hours. All of a sudden there was a noise in the brush. Father and son tensed. Not a muscle moved. Again the noise in the brush and they could see the antlers of a buck deer, then its head.

Without a word the father turned to the son. It was just his head that turned. Anything else would have made enough noise to send the animal scampering back into the safety of the woods. The son looked at the father. It was all in the eyes. The son didn't have to be told. It was plain enough in his father's eyes that this was the deer Jim had to shoot.

Jim looked down at his gun. He raised it to his shoulder, felt the trigger with his finger. He could feel his heart choke up with excitement. This wasn't just shooting at an old can. This wasn't shooting at an old box. There wasn't any practicing here. If he missed there wasn't going to be another shot at the deer. Maybe it would be a long time before his father would let him shoot again, if he missed. He mustn't miss. This was the test. His father was saying, "Go ahead. Let me see whether you're old enough or good enough to be a hunter."

Jim looked along the long barrel of his gun. He took his sight. He wasn't going to miss. He was going to show his father that he could be proud of his son, as proud as the son was of his father.

Jim took a quick, deep breath and held it, made sure of his sight.

He pulled the trigger.

There was a loud report. The deer looked startled, but only for a fraction of a second, and then dropped. Jim Thorpe had killed his first buck deer. He could feel his insides tremble. The blood rushed to his head, his fingers quivered on his gun with the sheer excitement, but young Jim gave no outward sign of the great joy and pride that welled up in him.

For a moment the father and son remained as they were, crouched and still, Jim waiting for his father to move first, to speak first. It wouldn't be like an Indian to do anything else. The impulse to jump up and down and shout, "I've got him! I've got him!" wasn't the thing a Sac and Fox did.

Father and son got to their feet together, almost as if a signal had been given. They walked together to the fallen deer. Only after he had examined the kill did Hiram speak.

"You will kill many deer," he said, simply.

That was all he needed to say. For Jim that was praise enough. More than that, it was the initiation into the tribe. He had won the right to sit with men and walk with men. He was acceptable to them. Most important, his father had accepted him. He was no longer a boy, he was a man. Yet Jim Thorpe was only ten years old.

When he was eight, Jim had gone camping out with

only his dog to keep him company. Now he could take his gun along, hunt the raccoon, track down the deer. The blood of his great ancestor, Chief Black Hawk of the Sac and Fox Indians, stirred in him.

Hunting game for food was only one of the chores of the reservation Indian. Each Indian in a family was entitled by the federal government to one hundred and sixty acres. The Thorpe family was a big one. Their land measured about twelve hundred acres and four to five hundred head of cattle grazed on it, besides the horses and the colts and the hogs. The Thorpes had a fairly large-sized ranch and it required a lot of hard work to keep it running in top order. Young Jim had to do his share. His particular job was feeding the live-stock, but he also pitched in when it came to breaking in the new flock of colts that appeared every year.

Jim didn't mind feeding the horses, the cows and the hogs, when they needed feeding, but he loved work-ing with the new and unbroken colts. By the time he was ten he could use the lasso like an expert and rope any wild colt that came within the range of his rope. Riding the colt was another matter. Getting onto the back of the young horse wasn't too difficult; but when the mad colt began to kick up its heel, twist, turn, stop suddenly and throw, more often than not the ten-year-old Jim would be sent sprawling to the ground where he would sit, chin in his hand, watching the frisky colt racing like the wind to the far end of the corral.

By the time he was fifteen, however, Jim says, "I

never met a wild one that I could not catch, saddle and ride. This was a great sport, and it made me strong and alert."

Everything Jim did as a boy made him strong and alert—the rough, tough games with his twin brother Charlie and the other boys on the reservation, the camping and hunting with his father, the chores on the ranch. It was all intensive and good training for the Jim Thorpe who was going to amaze the whole world with his great athletic prowess.

## three

WHEN JIM WAS six years old he was sent to the Sac and Fox reservation school of the district. The school was twenty-three miles away from the ranch, not a long distance in that part of our country, but Jim, with all the other children, was boarded there. Since twin brother Charlie was with him for the first two years, Jim didn't get too lonesome for the Thorpe homestead, the wild colts and the hunting trips with Big Hiram. He could always count the days to the holidays when he would be sent home. There was always the long summer vacation to go camping and trapping and fishing with the long spears. Besides, the boys at the school were like the boys at home. They played the same games Jim loved, wrestled, climbed trees and followed the leader. It was after Charlie died and Jim had to go off to school alone that leaving the ranch became harder. It took a lot of persuading to get Jim to go back to the reservation school after that first summer vacation without Charlie.

"I can help on the ranch," he argued. "You need me here."

But Big Hiram wanted his boy to get good book learning, a good education. No one could argue too long with Hiram.

Jim went to school all right, but his heart wasn't in it any more. He was always a "loner." He didn't make friends fast, no one could take Charlie's place. It was just before the end of his fourth year at the reservation school, in the springtime of the year when the grass is new-green and the air is fresh with the smell of new-growing things, that Jim's eyes began to wander more and more into the blue skies and across the plains and the big hills. He was only a little fellow. He wasn't quite ten. People who are much older get lonesome for home and the near ones they have left behind. Little Jim Thorpe, looking longer and longer toward the big ranch Hiram Thorpe ran, thinking of the colts that needed to be caught and broken, thinking of the fish teeming in the rivers, thinking of the wrestling matches in front of the Thorpe cabin every evening after the work was done, got homesick.

Early one morning after breakfast, without saying a word to any of his classmates, Jim simply walked out of the building, took a deep breath and began to walk quickly the long twenty-three miles home. He didn't walk the whole distance. Half the time he ran. He slowed up only when he got in sight of the Thorpe ranch.

He stopped, took it all in. It hadn't occurred to him to think of the kind of reception he was going to meet. He didn't know how his mother or father were going to feel about his coming home. He hadn't thought about it. There was a big grin on his face and all his insides were laughing. He was just a boy who was terribly happy to be coming home. And he wasn't a bit sorry to see his father waiting for him at the door.

Big Hiram, however, didn't seem to be as pleased as his young son. He looked at the boy, saw that there was nothing physically wrong with him, then waited for the young Jim to speak.

Hiram wasn't one to let on what he was thinking, but Jim saw at once that his father wasn't going to be very sympathetic about this running away from school.

"Did they throw you out?"

"I wanted to come home."

Big Hiram rubbed his chin. He was relieved that his son hadn't gotten himself disgraced.

"You wanted to come home," he repeated. "That's fine."

"I knew you'd understand," said Jim, but his tone wasn't too hopeful.

"You understand, too," said Hiram, "that I think a boy of your age ought to be in school, learning. And that's where you're going to be, in school, learning."

"You're not going to send me back?" pleaded Jim.

"No," said Hiram. "I'm not going to *send* you back. I'm going to *walk* you back."

And that's exactly what he did. He walked the boy back the twenty-three miles, deposited Jim at the door of the school, then turned around to trek the twenty-three miles back home.

Jim watched his father for a minute, waited till he disappeared behind a bend in the road. He took one look up at the school buildng, waved his hand good-by, then lit out across country for the home ranch.

This time Jim ran the whole distance. There was a short cut he knew. The country was rougher, the roads weren't too clear, but it was only eighteen miles instead of twenty-three. This time it was Jim who was at the door, waiting for his father to get home.

If Hiram was surprised, there was nothing in his Indian face to show it. Maybe he was even a little proud of his son's persistence. He didn't say anything about that either. He did say something, however, about Jim's schooling.

"This time," he announced very quietly, "I'm going to send you so far away from home you'll never be able to find your way back to the ranch."

And he did. He sent him to far-off Haskell Institute in Lawrence, Kansas. Haskell was a government school for Indians. It was here that Jim saw his first real baseball and football teams. It was here he met Chauncey Archiquette, an Indian who knew what to do with a pigskin once he got his hands on it.

Haskell had a pretty good team and Jim spent all the time he could watching the squad. He watched

Archiquette especially. His eager eyes never left him. He followed him, after scrimmage, the way any youngster follows a football hero.

"Can I touch that ball?" he asked, timidly.

"You can hold it, if you want to," said Archiquette.

Jim took it eagerly. His hands ran over the hide, as if it were the most precious thing in the world.

"Is this the way you hold it?"

"Just about," said Archiquette, smiling. "When your hands get bigger you'll be able to hold onto more of it."

Jim looked at his hero's big hands, compared them with his own.

"Maybe they'll be as big as yours someday."

"I'm sure they will," said the Haskell star. "You can give it a boot, if you want to try it."

Jim's eyes lit up.

"Sure," he said, looking gratefully up into the face of his hero. No one could have been prouder than Jim at that moment.

Everywhere Archiquette went, Jim would follow. The young Indian idolized the football player, worshiped him, tried to emulate him. He organized a team among his classmates, made a ball out of yarn, played the backfield against boys older and heavier than himself, and did a good job of it. Jim might have become a great Haskell star, but things turned out differently. One day a letter came to the head of the school. It carried bad news for Jim.

Jim didn't see the letter. The teachers kept it from him. But some other boys did see it.

"Your father's hurt."

"What are you talking about?"

"I read it in the office," said the well-meaning classmate. "He was shot. It was a hunting accident, the letter says. He's dying. They sent you the fare to go home."

Jim didn't wait for any more. He could see the whole picture clearly, his father lying in the small cabin, slowly bleeding to death. His head was in a whirl but no tears came to his eyes. Jim Thorpe was an Indian and an Indian does not display his pain or grief. Jim knew what had to be done, however, and he was going to do it. That night, no bag and no baggage, dressed only in his school overalls, he walked out of Haskell.

Outside of Lawrence he waited near the railroad yards for a train heading south. Soon a freight began to lumber out of the yards. He was in luck. There was an open door in one of the cars. The train began to pick up speed. Jim ran by its side, faster and faster and faster. And there was the open door. The young Jim leaped, got a hold, dragged himself in. For a moment he lay still, then looked around. The car was empty. He picked himself up, brushed off his overalls, looked out. He held his breath. The train wasn't moving south. It was going north. Quick as a flash, before the train gathered any more momentum, Jim leaped out, hit the ground hard, rolled, rolled, rolled, then lay still again.

I must have broken something, he thought. There was a twinge in his foot. He tried moving his toes, gently, then flexed his arch. It was sore but it wasn't broken. Slowly he got to his feet, felt all his muscles, ran his hand over his face. There was no blood.

"Lucky," said the Indian boy to himself.

He was bruised. He was well shaken up. He might have taken time out to nurse the aches in his arms and legs. Not Jim. He had a destination and he wanted to get there as quickly as he possibly could. Jim Thorpe started the long walk back home to Oklahoma.

Although that walk took Jim two weeks, the sight that met him was well worth the long trek. Hiram Thorpe wasn't dead and no bullet was going to kill him. He was far from the Big Hiram who could wrestle any man in the village down to the ground, but he wasn't going to die either.

"You sent for me," said Jim.

"Two weeks ago," said Hiram.

"It's a long way from Kansas to Oklahoma," said Jim. "Next time you won't send me quite that far, I hope."

But the gladness in the Thorpe homestead was not to last too long. Hiram got well but Charlotte, Jim's mother, was suddenly stricken with blood poisoning. It was only a few weeks after Jim got home that they buried his mother at the Sacred Heart Mission in Sacred

Heart, Oklahoma. The year was 1900. Jim was only twelve years old.

It was a severe blow to the Thorpe household. Charlotte was missed by the boys and the girls, and by Big Hiram, too. Tempers were sharp and Hiram impatient. One afternoon there was a bit of an argument between Hiram and Jim. Generally, Hiram could manage with a few well-chosen stern words. This time he gave his boys a good licking instead.

"I probably deserved it," says Jim, "but I didn't feel like taking it."

That afternoon, without a penny in his pockets, Jim set out for the tough Panhandle country in Texas. He was determined to show his father that even if he was only a boy he could stand up on his own two feet. Jim had much of the stubborn drive of his father's and more of the pride of both his father and his grandfather, Chief Black Hawk of the Fox and Sac Indians. He fixed fences on the range, he tamed wild horses. After a year away from home he had earned and saved enough to buy a team of horses.

"When I got back to Oklahoma with that team of horses," says Jim, "my father took one look at them and decided to take me back."

It wasn't just the horses which interested Big Hiram. He knew he had a son worthy of his name.

For the next three years Jim took up schooling again at the public school which was only three miles from the ranch. It was books and books and more books.

There was none of the football which had excited Jim so much at Haskell, no baseball, no track. It was all a pretty dull routine to Jim, who attended his classes more for his father's sake than for any other reason. At the end of those three years, however, when a traveling superintendent from Carlisle wandered down into the North Canadian River territory, the whole history of Jim's schooling changed.

"What do you want to be when you grow up?" asked the superintendent.

"An electrician."

The superintendent looked at the boy. He had never heard of an Indian being interested in electricity. It was a new experience for him. He was curious.

"We haven't got an electrical department," he said. "How would you like to learn to be a painter or a carpenter or a shoemaker?"

"I don't know," said Jim.

"You might try it."

Anything at the moment was better than the public school he had to go to. Besides, Pennsylvania was new territory.

"I'll try it," said Jim, and he signed up.

four

$C$APTAIN PRATT of the United States Army looked up at the hot midday sun. His eyes stretched back along the file of one hundred Indian prisoners he was moving across the country, from Fort Sill in Oklahoma to St. Augustine in Florida. He raised his right hand.

"Halt!" cried his lieutenant.

"At ease," said young Captain Pratt.

The line stopped. The soldiers rested on their guns. The Indian prisoners squatted where they had stopped. Captain Pratt dismounted, walked down the line and back again. He didn't say a word.

"Everything in order, sir?" asked his lieutenant.

"Everything," said Captain Pratt, but his lieutenant knew something was troubling his superior officer.

"Is there something, Captain. . ." he began.

The captain looked at his aide sharply.

"Yes, there's something." He spoke angrily. "There's something we ought to do for these Indians."

"Yes, sir," said the lieutenant, dutifully. He really didn't understand. This was almost one hundred years ago, when the Army was pretty busy putting down Indian uprisings throughout the West and the Southwest.

"There ought to be a government school," argued the young captain to the bewildered aide. "We ought to teach them trades, teach them the ways of the white men. They could be good citizens They could benefit themselves and benefit the communities in which they live."

"Yes, sir," said the lieutenant.

Captain Pratt turned to his younger aide. He saw the puzzled look in his face. There would be other puzzled faces but the captain would fight as hard for that school as he had fought the Indian warriors on the battefield.

He mounted his horse.

"Forward!" he ordered, and the line began to march.

It took many years and much heartache, but Captain Pratt's dream came true when finally, in 1879, an old deserted army post became the Carlisle Indian School.

Jim was fifteen whe he reported to Carlisle in 1904. He was only a little over five feet tall and weighed a skimpy one hundred and fifteen. There wasn't anything resembling a football uniform that wouldn't swim on him, but the game fascinated him. His eyes lit up as he watched the ball snapped back from center in varsity-scrub battles. His muscles tensed with the back carrying the pigskin. His shoulders ached to get into the melee, to throw a smashing block, to bull his way down the field. This was a tough game, the competition keen. It called for stamina, for quick thinking, for sheer strength. Jim couldn't wait for the height and weight he needed to get into the middle of it. When the whistle blew for the end of the drill, Jim was as exhausted as any of the players leaving the gridiron. He lived through every run, every kick, every smashing play he had seen and followed.

It would be three years before Jim Thorpe, standing five feet eleven and a half inches and tipping the scale at one hundred and eighty-one, would really begin to play the grueling game, and much was to happen in those three years.

It was only two months after he had arrived at Carlisle that Jim got the heart-breaking news that his father had died. The blood poisoning that had carried away his mother had killed his greatest love. Jim couldn't even get back to Oklahoma in time for the burial.

"Sorry, Jim," said his teachers.

"Thanks," said Jim, quietly.

"Sorry," said his classmates who had heard the news.

"Thanks," said Jim, and he walked out into the fields at night, to be alone with his memories and his sorrow. First it had been his twin, Charlie, who had been everything a brother could be. Then it was his mother. Now it was the man in whose footsteps he wanted to follow, Big Hiram who had been champion over all the other Indians on the ranch, who was gone. Although there were others at home, except for his older brother George there was no one he had been close to. Even George had drifted away from him. Young Jim Thorpe felt all alone in the world. He was still only a very young lad. But he did not weep. Charlie, his mother, his father were no longer with him but he would make good for all of them.

"I'll fight it out alone," he said into the night, with a savage determination. "I'll fight it alone."

Then he softened and added, "I know you'll always be with me, Dad."

Schoolwork helped Jim take his mind off Oklahoma, but he never forgot his childhood, Charlie, his mother or his father, Big Hiram.

At the end of his first term at Carlisle he was sent to live and work with a Pennsylvania Dutch family in Summerdale, Pennsylvania. This was part of the school program. He was to work around the house, learn how to cook and get five dollars a month for his labors. The plan was a good one but not for Jim. He didn't mind the work but he didn't enjoy being kept indoors. H resented havng to eat in the kitchen away from th rest of the family. He tried. He disciplined his urge to get out into the wind and the rain and the sunshine, but the pride of the young Sac and Fox couldn't take the business of being relegated to the kitchen. He was as good as any man and better than some. The blood of men who had fought and died for freedom and equality coursed in his veins.

"I would like to be transferred," he wrote to Carlisle. "I want to work outdoors and I want to sit as an equal with the other members of the family I work with."

It was the voice of generations of Indians who had sat together as equals before the ceremonial fires and smoked the pipe of peace together, all men alike and all men respected as brothers.

His request was granted.

For the next two years Jim worked on farms, earned eight dollars a month and ate with the man who had hired him. At the end of two years Jim was nineteen, ready to return to Carlisle to meet the man who was to start him on the road to the greatest athletic career in the story of American sports.

The first to really notice the great possibilties in the Indian was a man who has been pretty much forgotten. He was an assistant coach at the school. His name was Newman.

"Who's the boy who made that tackle?"

He was watching the Tailors' team playing the Carpenters' squad. The boys who couldn't make varsity organized a sectional league for the school. Jim was playing guard for the Tailors.

"Thorpe," said one of the boys on the bench. "Jim Thorpe."

Newman didn't hear him. He was watching the boy as he cut through the line, sure, certain, watched him

nail the runner before he could get his feet in motion.
He watched him block, run, kick. He watched him
all afternoon.

"You're pretty good, young fellow," he said, as the
boys came trotting off the field.

"Thanks," said Jim, quietly. "I guess I like the
game."

"I can see that," said Newman. "Report to the
scrubs tomorrow."

Jim just looked at the coach. He could feel his heart
beating fast.

"Aren't you going to say anything?" asked Newman.

Jim struggled to loosen his tongue. He never could
release his feelings in a flow of words.

"Sure, Coach," he said. "I'll be there"

And he was there all right, but Glen Scobie Warner,
Pop Warner, one of the greatest track and football
coaches of all time, took a little while in recognizing
the great potentialities of the new boy Assistant Coach
Newman had sent on to his scrub squad. It was on the
track field and not on the gridiron that Jim Thorpe
first excited the man whose fame was to grow almost
step for step with the Indian's swift rise to athletic glory.

Jim had been playing a pickup game of ball, as he
often did after the day's classes. On the way back to
school he crossed the field where some members of the
track team were practicing high jumping. He stopped
to watch them. Anything that involved athletic competition interested Jim. He had never done any high

jumping but that didn't mean that he wouldn't like to try it.

The bar was set at five feet when the track team started its jumping. Five feet was easy. Everyone could do it. They jumped five feet two and five feet three inches easily, too. It was when the bar was raised to five feet six that the casualties began. There were only four or five who could manage that. There were three who could jump five feet seven without spilling the bar. Only two could go any higher. Then the bar was lifted to five feet nine.

First one tried it. He stepped back about ten yards, got up on his toes, took the few strides to the bar and leaped. When he came down, the bar came down with him.

Then the second Indian tried it. The short run, the leap and down he came—and the bar with him.

They tried it again and again and again. They got up there all right, the five feet nine, but when they came down, the stick was down, too. They were about to give up, lower the bar for some more practice jumps, when Jim, who had waited patiently by, asked whether he couldn't try.

"Go ahead," said one of the boys who had managed to clear the bar at five feet eight. "Careful you don't break your neck."

"Thanks," said Jim, all eager to get his feet off the ground. He didn't notice the smiles on the faces of the Carlisle high jumpers.

"If a horse can do it," he announced, solemnly, "I guess I can do it, too."

But there was something thoroughly serious about the young Indian, despite his quip. The boys turned to watch him. Among them, unnoticed by Jim, was Coach Warner.

Thorpe took his proper distance, looked at the bar once, made the short run and leaped. It was the most beautiful leap anyone had ever seen at the Indian school. There was daylight, plenty of daylight between those tailor shop overalls and the bar set at five feet nine. And when Jim came down on the other side of it, the stick stayed right where it had been placed.

Jim looked back at the bar and grinned.

"It wasn't too hard at that," he said. Nothing would ever be too hard for Jim in any sport, in any athletic competition.

The boys of the track team were struck too dumb to answer, their eyes and mouths wide open as they watched the Indian nonchalantly walk back toward the school grounds.

The next afternoon Jim was called in by Coach Warner.

"Anything wrong?" asked the anxious young Indian.

Warner scratched his head. This innocence was something new for him.

"Are those the overalls you wore when you jumped yesterday?"

"Yes, sir. Is that bad?"

"And you were wearing those tennis shoes?"

"Yes, sir. I haven't gotten into any trouble, have I?"

"Listen, Thorpe," said Warner, poking his finger into Jim's chest. "In a track uniform and with spiked shoes you'll be jumping six feet."

"I can do that now," said Jim. "At least I think I can."

"I'll bet you can," agreed the smiling coach. "You report to the track team."

"I can't, sir."

Warner scowled.

"Why not?"

"I'm playing with the Hotshots."

The scrub team was called the Hotshots by the boys of Carlisle.

"I'd like to finish the season," explained Thorpe.

Warner smiled.

"So you play football, too?"

"Yes, sir."

"Funny I haven't noticed you around."

"Perhaps you will now," said the blunt young Indian.

"Perhaps," said Coach Warner.

He did.

## five

$T$HERE were about fifty linemen all over the gridiron. Pop Warner placed them five feet apart, guards, tackles, ends, centers—and a few backfield men were there, too, to plug up any holes. He gave the ball to young Thorpe.

"Here! Let's see how far *you* can carry it?"

Thorpe tucked the pigskin under his arm. He was standing under the goal posts. His eyes stretched over the field of big Indians, all eyes glued on him, ready to drop him with a single savage thrust as soon as he hit their territory. He looked out at the goal posts across the gridiron, one hundred long yards away.

He looked back to the big-browed, square-chinned Glenn Warner.

"Now?" he asked.

"Now," said Pop Warner.

The young Indian clutched the ball, his head went deep into his shoulders and he was off, all muscles and determination, running, swerving, sprinting. A tackle hit him and bounced back. A guard knifed at his hips but there were no hips to grip and the guard sprawled out on the turf. Down the field went Thorpe, ducking, side-stepping, leaving center, tackle, end, guard clutching at the thin air where a ball carrier was supposed to be. Ten men more, eight, six, four—and Jim was in the clear. There was a frown on Pop Warner's face as the Indian crossed the last chalk mark on the field. His linemen couldn't be that bad. There was a big grin on Jim Thorpe's broad face. He liked this running with the pigskin. It was a good game. It was fun tucking that ball under his arm, threading, banging his way to the other end of the field, over the goal.

"Come here with that ball!" yelled Coach Warner.

"Yes, sir," said the still-grinning Thorpe.

Pop Warner took the ball, looked at the Indian.

"This is tackling practice!" he barked. "Understand?"

The grin dropped from Jim's mouth. He had made a good run. He hadn't expected the coach to give him any medals for it, but he didn't see any reason to be yelled at either.

"Nobody tackles Jim," he said grimly.

Warner looked at the boy. He knew the Indian boys at Carlisle had grit, courage. He knew they were fired with a special quality of pride which would never admit defeat. Sometimes it was important for the morale of these boys to show them that they were as vulnerable as the next fellow, that it was no disgrace to be hit by an opposing guard, even thrown behind the scrimmage lines for a loss.

"Do you want to try it again?" he asked.

"Sure," said Jim, still dead pan.

"Take it!" said Warner, shoving the ball into his ribs.

Jim stood at the goal line. He listened to Warner bark his instructions to the field.

"Hit him! And hit him hard! Hit him and bring him down! That's what you're here for! If you can't stop the man with the ball, turn in your uniforms! Understand? I don't want anybody here who is afraid to hit the dirt!"

He turned to Thorpe.

"All right! Let's see you do it again!"

Jim gripped the ball. He took one look at all the boys down the field, priming to hit him. "Nobody is going to tackle Jim," he said to himself, and down the field he went. A tackle lunged and hit nothing. A guard ripped at him savagely and hit nothing. Three linemen hit him and bounced off, as if they had hit a stone wall. There was no one to stop Jim Thorpe.

He crossed the goal line on his two feet and handed the pigskin to Coach Warner.

"Nobody tackles Jim," he repeated and walked off to the side lines.

Warner lifted the peak of his cap, scratched his head with amazement.

"He sure is one wild Indian," he said, but he didn't ask anyone on the gridiron to turn in his uniform. That was the year Glenn Warner had Albert Payne playing in the Carlisle backfield, Exendine at end and Hauser right halfback. It was one of the really great teams Warner coached during his sixteen years at the Indian school, and Glenn was as proud of his athletes as they were of him.

Warner, himself, had been a great guard for Cornell where he had played in 1892, 1893 and 1894. In 1894 he had captained Camp's All-America. He coached Georgia to an unbeaten, untied record in 1896, then went up to coach the Cornell team to a ten-win, two-loss record in 1898. One of the Cornell wins that year was against Carlisle.

"We outscored them," said Warner, "but we didn't defeat them."

He admired the spirit of the Indians, their toughness, their stamina and unwillingness to give up. When things got uncomfortable at Cornell and it looked as though he were going to lose his job there, it was a pretty happy Glenn Warner who accepted a bid from Carlisle to teach and coach its determined and valiant warriors. He might have gone to Minnesota. The two bids came to him on the same day. Warner chose the Indian school and he wasn't to regret it. In his very first year there, 1899, with Isaac Seneca of the New York Seneca tribe of Indians playing halfback, Carlisle mopped up the tough eastern teams and then traveled to the Pacific Coast to beat the vaunted University of California by the score of 2 to 0.

It was at Carlisle that Glenn Warner became the first coach to number his players' shirts for the benefit of the fans, where he introduced the famous reverse play, developed his single and double wing back systems, the crouch start and the clipping block. The greatest Warner discovery, however, was just beginning to learn the game that afternoon he ran through a field full of would-be tacklers. The greatness of Thorpe as all-time All-America was still a few years off.

In 1907 Jim rode the bench for most of the season and he didn't like it. He was restless. He couldn't sit still. He was always jumping up and down on the field. It was all right, watching a smash off tackle, a long end run, a hard block or a long punt, but he hadn't got himself on the football squad just to watch. He wanted to play the game. He wanted to get his hands on the ball, carry it, make that touchdown. Jim wasn't cut out to sit on the side lines. He was born and bred a fighter and where there was a fight he belonged in the middle of it.

He got his chance at Franklin Field. Pennsylvania had a good, tough team. They were hitting the Carlisle Indians with everything they had. It was a clean game but a rough one. Five minutes after the opening kick-off, Albert Payne, the Klamath Indian, lay stretched on the ground, clutching a painful knee. He had to be helped off the field.

Glenn Warner turned to the boys on the bench.

Payne was a brilliant left halfback. It wasn't going to be easy to fill his shoes. He looked at Thorpe. The boy's eyes fixed themselves eagerly on the coach.

"All right," signaled Warner.

Jim was up on his feet but he didn't move.

"What are you waiting for?" snapped the coach.

Jim wanted to say, "Thanks," but he couldn't. His mouth opened but no words came. He never could say in words the deep feelings that moved him. He just shoved his helmet down on his head and streaked out onto the field. It didn't matter to Jim that he didn't know half the signals. He was going to play. That was the important thing.

"Let me carry the ball," he whispered to the quarterback. "I'll run it for you."

The quarterback looked over the eager substitute for the injured Payne, he called the signals. Jim got the ball all right, but he didn't run it. Not this time. Before he could find his interference the whole Penn line was down on him. When the referee put the ball down, Carlisle had lost five yards.

"I thought you were going to run it," said the quarterback.

"Next time," said the undaunted Jim. "Give it to me again." His eyes were steel points of determination. "They won't touch me next time," he insisted. "Let me have it."

"66 . . . 77 . . . 24 . . . ."

Jim was going to carry it. He was on his toes.

"48 . . . 76 . . . ."

The ball came back from center into Jim's big hands, then out across the field went the Indian, the pigskin under his arm, swerving, ducking, side-stepping, sprinting, bowling over every man who came near him, every man who tried to stop him. Seventy-five yards from scrimmage he carried that ball to a touchdown. There wasn't a hand within twenty yards of him as he stroked across the Penn line.

"Shades of Isaac Seneca," said Pop Warner to himself as he counted the Penn men sprawled all over Franklin Field.

"Great!" said the boys of Carlisle, pounding the back of their new star. "Where have you been, Thorpe? Where have you been hiding?"

Jim grinned, fighting his way back across the gridiron.

"That was fun," he said. "Give it to Jim again."

There were two men in the Pennsylvania line that afternoon who made Walter Camp's All-American first team, Draper at tackle and Ziegler at guard. There was Scarlett at end and Hollenback at halfback who made Camp's All-American second team. But Penn was no match for Carlisle's Indian boys in that game that introduced Thorpe.

They kept feeding the ball to Jim, and although Jim hadn't played the game long enough to know how to fake a man out of position, he just ran too fast for the tackle to hit him. He didn't know that he ought to be hugging the side lines, he just bulled his way through the opposition until he was in the clear. The great squad that played for Pennsylvania couldn't find him half the time, and when they found him they just bounced off.

Carlisle smothered the Penn team 26-6.

"The greatest team I ever had," says Pop Warner today, "was that Carlisle team of 1907."

They beat Harvard, the University of Minnesota, champion of the Western Conference, and Chicago, among others. They lost only to Princeton on a field of mud.

"He was still just a growing boy," says Pop Warner, recalling the first football Thorpe played for him. "He was inclined to be lazy, didn't like to practice. He never went all out in the game except when he felt like it. And that was about forty per cent of the time. Football was just a good time to Jim. I never saw him snarl. Most of the time he just laughed, talked to the boys on the other team, enjoyed himself. But of course you couldn't keep him down on the bench. That bench was never made for Jim. He had a natural change of pace that just floated him past the defense. His reactions were so fast that sometimes you couldn't follow him with the naked eye. Punishment didn't mean a thing to him. He was fearless and he hit so hard that the other fellow was always getting the bruises."

Jim wasn't a one-man football team, but he was to become the most feared, the most respected, the greatest player to ever carry a pigskin out onto the gridiron. There never has been a man who could kick, block and run the way Jim Thorpe did for that little Indian school of Carlisle.

*I*N 1908, THE SPRING following his great start in football, Jim Thorpe began to throw his weight around on the track and in all the field events that go along with a track meet.

"If you can jump five feet ten," said Coach Warner, pushing up the stick for his high jump squad, "I'll take you along to the Penn relays."

Jim edged the stick up another notch.

"Let's make it a little harder," he said.

Pop Warner just watched him.

The Indian shrugged his shoulders, stepped back the ten yards, took his few running strides, sailed up into the air and cleared the bar with inches to spare.

Coach Warner still said nothing.

Jim picked himself up from the turf, examined the markings on the poles.

"That was five feet eleven," he said, simply. "Shall I push it up some more."

Glenn Warner studied his boy intently for a moment, and then he burst out:

"Push it up to six feet! You weren't even trying!"

"Do I have to try, too?" came back Jim, who never put himself out except when he really felt like it. "That ought to be enough to win the meet, don't you think?"

"I won't tell you what I think," snapped Warner. "You just keep pushing that stick up!"

And Jim did.

At the Penn games, Jim cleared the bar at six feet one. It was good enough to tie for first place.

An official flipped a coin in the air.

"Call!"

"Head!" cried Jim, watching the coin spin down.

"Head!" said the official.

"Mine!" said Jim.

It was a beautiful medal. That first medal is always a beautiful medal. Jim shined it up, shined it up again. He liked medals. He was going to win a lot more before he would turn in his spiked shoes.

There was a meet in Harrisburg. There was a meet in Philadelphia. Jim placed first in the broad jump. He placed first in the low hurdles and then in the high hurdles. He placed first again in the high jump. Jim Thorpe won plenty of medals that first year of his as a regular on the Carlisle track team. It was the beginning of a great collection.

At an A.A.U. meet he stopped to watch some of the

really brawny fellows tossing a heavy object down the field.

"What's that you're throwing?" he asked, curious.

"Hammer."

For a couple of minutes he kept watching as the big muscle boys took turns at hurling the weight.

"Can't get it over that 140-foot mark, can you?" he said at last.

One of the boys picked up the 16-pound weight.

"Want to try it?" he asked.

Jim wasn't bashful about these things.

"Sure."

He examined the hammer as if it were a new kind of toy, looked out to the 140-foot mark.

"Is this the way you do it?" he asked.

But he wasn't expecting an answer and he didn't get one. He just stepped up to the mark and in perfect form, as if he had been practicing for years, effortlessly hurled the weight one hundred and forty-five feet.

The hammer throwers were a little too stunned to make any speeches about it. Not Jim Thorpe.

"It isn't any harder than it looks," he said, and hammer tossing became another medal winner for the great Indian.

Running, high-jumping, pole-vaulting, hurdling, hammer-throwing would certainly be enough of a program for any good athlete. Jim had time for baseball, basketball, tennis, lacrosse. And when he wasn't pitching for the Carlisle Indians or taking a turn in the infield or involved in any one of the other games, he went in for gymnastics or swimming. There was no athletic competition at the Indian school that didn't find Jim Thorpe in the middle of it. There was no sport in which Jim Thorpe wasn't top notch.

The 1908 Carlisle eleven had Jim playing halfback from its first scrimmage. Although it wasn't the best squad in the country, it was good enough to hold an unbeaten Penn squad with its All American Hollenback, Scarlett and Miller to a 6-6 tie. It was Jim Thorpe who scored that tying touchdown in one of the toughest games ever played on the gridiron. Carlisle won ten games that year, lost two, tied one. Jim Thorpe made Walter Camp's third team All-America. He was still a few years away from football immortality.

It was in the spring of 1909 that the Indian really began to burn up the cinder paths as few Americans have ever done or ever will do. He became almost a one-man track team all by himself. He was a streak in the sprints, a record breaker on the field. There was no event he could not enter; and if he entered an event the chances were that he would win it.

Harold Anson Bruce, who was later to coach the Austrian Olympic team, had a powerful track squad at Lafayette. He had invited the Indians, who had made a pretty good reputation for themselves, to a dual meet in celebration of that college's Alumni Day.

Coach Warner accepted the invitation but asked for a steep guarantee.

"Nonsense," said Coach Bruce and he tossed the message from Carlisle into the basket.

But the idea of an Indian-Lafayette meet was his own little dream child. He fished the letter out of the basket, walked all around town, talked to every businessman he could collar, every shopkeeper, every alumnus, and he collected that guarantee Glenn Warner wanted.

He wired his O.K. to Carlisle and then began to fret. If anything went wrong, if the meet were to turn out a flop, there would be only one man to shoulder the indignation of all the townspeople who had dipped into their pockets for that Warner guarantee. Harold Anson Bruce began to worry. He almost collapsed when he met the Indian team which had come to compete with his forty-six-man crack squad.

On the day of the scheduled meet, Bruce appointed himself a one-man reception committee, and one hour before the train was due he went down to the railroad station to meet it.

Those were long minutes he counted as he paced up and down the platform, chewing his nails. He had visions of a whole tribe of redskins pouring out of the coaches. He saw them stampeding down through the town and onto the college grounds. He could hear the war-whooping of hundreds—thousands—of mad, wild, war-painted braves storming into the quiet citadel.

Coach Anson was a mass of sweat as he watched the train finally pull into the station.

A couple of men got off at one end of the platform, a few at the other end. From the middle car came only one big, broad-shouldered individual with a slouch hat pulled over his eyes. That was Coach Warner.

Anson went limp. Where were the Indians? A horde of savages descending on Lafayette was bad enough. But no savages was worse.

"Where are your Indians?" he shouted.

Glenn Warner looked at the hysterical Anson, lifted his hat from his head.

"They'll be here," he said, looking out toward the college grounds. "They'll be here."

Bruce wiped the sweat from his head. Pop Warner was chewing on a straw. Bruce would have liked to pull the straw right out of his mouth.

"Where are they?" he asked.

"What are you worried about my Indians for?" asked Warner, tossing the straw away. "They're coming, I told you."

"Listen, Warner," said Bruce, pleading. "I had to go all over Easton raising a public subscription to meet your guarantee. We've advertised the Indians all over Lehigh Valley. I have a strong team of forty-six athletes and you don't seem to have any. And there are fourteen events on the program. Pop, how many Indians will you have?"

Warner shifted the hat on his head.

"Five," he said.

Bruce almost passed out. He saw all Easton at his throat, clamoring for his hide.

"Five!" he shouted.

"You don't think you can beat me, do you?" asked Warner.

Bruce just stared, aghast, and Pop Warner reached into his pocket, pulled out a roll of big bills.

"Do you want to make a little bet?"

"My Lord!" whispered Bruce, hoarsely.

But that wasn't the end of the interview.

"Harold," pursued Pop Warner, "if it isn't going to make too much trouble for you, I wish you would run this meet off fast. We'd like to catch the four forty-six train out of here tomorrow."

Bruce just looked at his opposing coach, too choked up to answer that one.

The morning of the meet was bright with sunlight and the new-mown green grass was sweet with all the smells of spring, but Coach Bruce was not in tune with nature. He kept thinking of the terible beating in store for the five Indian boys from Carlisle—and the beating that was going to be his after the races were all run. He was far from a happy man as he sent his squad against the small Carlisle team.

In the half-mile Arquett and Tewanima, Indians from Carlisle, ran one-two and Bruce allowed himself a breath. It wasn't going to be a complete runaway for Lafayette, a farce. That's what worried him most. He was deathly afraid the whole meet would turn out to be the biggest joke he had ever played on himself.

In the mile the two Indian boys, Arquett and Tewanima, again ran one-two. Coach Bruce began to take notice.

In the two-mile Arquett and Tewanima repeated the one-two trick and Coach Harold Anson Bruce stopped worrying about the poor five-man squad from Carlisle. He began to worry about the forty-six-man squad of Lafayette.

The Indian's Shenandoah took the high hurdles and came in second in the low hurdles. Johnson of Carlisle ran away with the quarter. The fifth man of the five-man squad was young Jim Thorpe. He put the finishing touches to Lafayette and to Coach Bruce.

In the hundred-yard dash the Indian ran second. That was just a warm-up. He took all the rest, the pole vault, the high jump, the low hurdles, the shot-put and the broad jump.

Coach Bruce was a sick man when they ran up the totals. The great forty-six-man Lafayette track team had amassed a grand total of thirty-one points. The little squad of five men from the Indian school had collected seventy-one points and the meet. It was just plain, unadulterated slaughter.

Glenn Warner and his Indian boys had no trouble catching the four forty-six out of Easton—with the guarantee.

Those boys could run any track team into the

ground. There were eight of them when they traveled
up to Syracuse to take on Tom Keane's squad of forty
to fifty great athletes. Pop Warner, evidently rating
Syracuse a couple of notches above Lafayette, added
three men to his team. It was a good squad, but the
Carlisle Indians were better. Jim Thorpe carried away
five firsts, one second and two thirds in the meet.
Carlisle won by one point. That was close for the small
Indian squad which included Louis Tewanima who
was to become a great ten-thousand-meter star in the
1912 Olympic games at Stockholm, and the greatest
of them all, Jim Thorpe.

## seven

SCHOOL WAS OVER for the season and Jim was packing his grips, slowly, aimlessly. Everybody else was going home or to some job he had lined up, but Jim was going nowhere. He didn't want to go back to Oklahoma. There would be no Big Hiram to greet him and Oklahoma was no longer home without him. Even the memory of his father was enough to pull Jim miles away from the people all around him.

"I don't know where I'm going," he said, and he wasn't talking to anybody in particular. He was just remembering the day his father gave him a gun, the day his father said, "That deer is yours."

"Why don't you come along with us?" asked Jesse Young Deer, a boy who was pretty handy with a baseball glove and bat.

"They can use us down in Carolina, I hear," chipped in Joe Libby, another good ballplayer. "And they pay you for playing," he added.

Jim hesitated.

"Going back to the farm?" needled Young Deer.

"What's wrong with the farm?"

"Nothing. Except you might have more fun banging out the old baseball."

Jim thought for a minute.

"I'll go along for the ride," he said. The ride was all he meant.

The Rocky Mount Club in North Carolina took a look at the Indian boys, watched them toss the ball around the infield, watched them take their cuts at the ball. The manager of the club was impressed.

"I can use all three of you."

"How much are you going to pay us?" asked Jesse Young Deer. He was all business. A lot of the college boys were playing ball during the summer and some of them were getting a neat sum for it.

"Fifteen dollars a week," said the manager. "Take it or leave it."

Fifteen dollars a week was a big deal for the Indian boys.

"I'll take it," said Joe Libby.

"Count me in, too," said Jesse Young Deer.

"How about you?" asked the Rocky Mount manager, turning to Jim Thorpe.

"I'm just watching," said Jim, "if it doesn't make any difference to you."

"Suit yourself," said the manager and Jim watched, but not for long.

He had a little money when he left Carlisle but that went fast. It wasn't long before he was talking himself into a job with the Rocky Mount Club.

"It's fifteen dollars a week," said the manager. "Same as the other boys."

He handed him an infield mitt.

"You'll play third base."

The first game Jim played for the club was against Raleigh. His arm was strong. He could whip the ball across the diamond like a bullet. He was accurate, too, and that was even more important.

"How would you like to pitch?" the manager asked him one morning.

"Anything you say," said the indifferent Indian.

And he pitched.

"Just get them over the plate," said the manager.

"Shall I let them hit the ball?" asked the fearless Indian.

The manager just looked at the boy.

"Get them over the plate," he said. "That's all I'm asking."

For three innings Jim didn't give a hit. His ball was streaking over the plate so fast the batter couldn't see it, or it was dancing a jig so that the batsman didn't know which way it was coming or going. The manager watched without comment. He had seen too many youngsters start like a house on fire and then fizzle out fast.

For six . . . for seven innings Jim didn't allow a runner to cross the plate. He was getting stronger all the time.

"Did you ever pitch before?" asked the slightly bewildered manager.

"Once in a while," said Jim, laconically.

The manager scratched his head. These Indians sure are funny people, he thought. They certainly don't talk much.

Jim never did talk much but he didn't have to talk. His pitching did all his talking for him. While the manager of the Rocky Mount Club watched with growing wonder, the young Indian boy continued to pour the ball across the plate. He was good enough that afternoon to win a 4-0 shutout. He was good enough to win twenty-three games out of the twenty-five he pitched for the Rocky Mount Club in that first season of his in professional baseball.

The next summer he was with Rocky Mount again. Word of his great pitching had spread and the National League Boston Braves sent a man down to North Carolina to scout him out. But Jim had strained his arm, pitching game after game. They used him as a starter for Rocky Mount but they didn't hesitate to send him in to relieve a wabbling pitcher, and with no regard for that great wing of his. When the Boston scout arrived on the scene it was too late. Jim was never going to be a great pitcher again.

From Rocky Mount he moved on to Fayetteville and then to Arkansas. It was while he was with the Arkansas club that the whole league collapsed, and Jim went home to Oklahoma pretty much discouraged with organized baseball. He had never earned more than sixty dollars a month playing the game, and that sixty dollars was going to cause him the greatest disappointment in his great athletic career.

He had been away from Carlisle for two years. Back home in Oklahoma his thoughts turned to the Indian school and to Pop Warner, to the high jumping and the hurdling, to the pigskin he loved to hold. He had made a mistake, he knew, when he left Carlisle to play ball with Jesse Young Deer and Joe Libby. He would have liked to live those years over again. He wouldn't repeat the error. He had given up too much—he knew even then—for the games he had played for Rocky Mount.

He looked at his medals, polished them and put them away. His days at Carlisle he felt were all over, never to be recaptured. It was an almost ecstatic Jim Thorpe who one day, back in 1911, eagerly opened a letter from Coach Glenn Scobie Warner.

## eight

"COME BACK TO CARLISLE," wrote Glenn Warner. "Start training and I think you can make the Olympic team that goes to Stockholm."

Thorpe didn't need any coaxing. Despite his brilliant record, he hadn't made any real friendships in Rocky Mount. There was no one to keep him in Oklahoma. He packed his things, said his good-byes and headed straight back to the Indian school.

"Where have you been all this time?" asked Warner.

"Just playing ball," said Jim, easily.

Pop didn't stop to ask where he had played ball or how; he was giving his crack athlete the once-over, feeling mighty good about his return to Carlisle. Jim stood over six feet one now, and he was a trim one hundred and eighty-five pounds. He was a mature man with a barrel chest, thick neck and jutting jaw. Glenn Warner, still chewing on a straw, looked his boy over and was well satisfied with the results.

"You're just in time to get into a football uniform," he said, struggling hard to conceal the wind Jim's return had put into his sails. "We can start training for the Olympics after the season."

Although Jim hadn't been near a football for almost two years, the pigskin nestled warmly in his big hands like something born to them.

"Glad you're back with us," said the Carlisle boys, gathering around the big man. "We can use you."

Jim just grinned.

They gave Jim the ball in a scrimmage drill and he went through the line as if it were made up of children's blocks. He kicked the ball and it went almost the distance of the gridiron. He threw a block and they had to help the would-be tackler off the field.

"This is just practice, Jim," complained a teammate.

"Sorry," said Jim, but there was a big grin on his face, and his teammate grinned and slapped his back.

"We sure are glad you're playing for Carlisle," he said.

Jim Thorpe had been a star in 1909, but there weren't enough adjectives to describe the greatness of the Indian in 1911.

Glenn Warner sent him into the game against Dickinson, the first clash of the season, for only seventeen minutes. In those seventeen minutes the Indian scored seventeen points. It was just a whisper of what was to come.

Against St. Mary's he blasted the opposition with

such brutal force that Pop Warner had to pull him out of the game before he killed somebody. In that game Thorpe scored fifteen points with three touchdowns. A touchdown scored only five points in those days.

Against Georgetown, the first tough opposition Carlisle faced that season, Thorpe was merciless, blasting and hammering his way through the line of the eleven which was supposed to take Carlisle fairly easily.

The press sat up and took notice. However, the gridiron experts were not yet ready to concede the greatness of the team which played for the Indian school.

"While Carlisle has a fine team and one of the best backfield men in the East in Thorpe, the Braves are stepping out of their class against such powerhouses as Pittsburgh, Harvard, Army and Syracuse."

That's what one newspaperman wrote. Others were even less polite. And they were all ready to write, "I told you so," when the sixteen-man squad from Carlisle turned up for the Pittsburgh game.

"They've got us licked," said Pop Warner to his boys in the dressing room. He knew their psychological make-up better than anybody else.

"Who has?" asked the indignant Jim Thorpe. He never bothered to read the press clippings.

"All the newspapermen," said Warner.

"Is that so?" demanded an aroused Thorpe.

"That's so," said the coach, quietly.

"Well, we'll show them!" shouted the Indian.

And he did.

They were laying for Thorpe. On every play, two, three, four Panthers out of Pittsburgh cracked into him. When he went down they piled onto him. Hands, arms, legs, elbows, knees—they gave him everything they could. They wanted him out of the game, and they wanted him out fast.

Jim, always a good-natured fellow, wasn't ruffled. Every time he got back to his feet he flashed that big, friendly grin at them.

"Right tackle," he shouted so the Panthers could hear him, and through right tackle he went.

"Center," he shouted for the benefit of the opposing linemen, and right through center like a shot out of a cannon, he crashed.

All afternoon he dared them to stop him, but there was no stopping Jim Thorpe. His stiff arm went out like a piston, turning tackler after tackler around like a top, dropping them in their tracks. He bulled his way through the line, smashed through the secondary. Carlisle romped off with a 17-0 victory.

"That Thorpe is everything they say about him," wrote one sports writer, taking his hat off to the Indian, "and more."

Lafayette was beaten 19-0. Jim's kicking in the game was phenomenal. He averaged seventy yards on his boots.

Jim walked with crutches for the whole week after that Lafayette game, but it didn't stop him from donning his uniform to beat Pennsylvania 16-0. There was nothing wrong with those legs when the chips were down.

The biggest game of the year was the classic with Harvard. Percy Haughton was Harvard's coach. His team had won eight straight games. The Big Three, Yale, Princeton and Harvard, dominated football in those days, the way Notre Dame dominated football in recent seasons. They had the pick of all the best prep schools and their reputation alone was enough to paralyze the opposition. The 1911 team the Carlisle Indians went to meet boasted Fisher, All-American guard; Wendell, All-American halfback; Smith at end, Reynolds, Storer—enough weight and brains to scare any normal squad of football players. Carlisle Indians, however, were not ordinary gridiron material. They never frightened.

Cambridge Stadium was jammed. Twenty-five thousand people had come out to see what little Carlisle would do against the powerful John Harvard. Thorpe was a national hero by this time. He had captured the public's imagination and they half wanted to see the Indian boys win the battle against the mighty Ivy League team. They felt, however, it was a hopeless task. The odds heavily favored the much stronger squad from Cambridge.

Percy Haughton, whose eleven ran three deep and who hadn't been impressed by stories about Thorpe and the Indians, started his second squad. And early in the very first period they pushed over a touchdown and kicked the extra point. With their quick lead of 6-0, it looked like a walkaway for the Johnny Harvards to every one sitting in the stadium—and Haughton was all smiles.

Carlisle managed to get the ball down to the Harvard twenty-yard line but their attack stalled. Thorpe, his legs all taped, wasn't running.

"Let me carry it," he demanded.

"We need you in here, Jim," argued his teammates. "You can't run. Your legs are all banged up."

"Give me the ball," insisted Thorpe.

"You can kick it," urged his quarterback.

"I'll kick it," said Thorpe.

And he did. From the twenty-third-yard line, bad legs and all, he booted the ball between the uprights. Score: Harvard 6, Carlisle 3. A faint hope stirred among the twenty-five thousand spectators, not for victory but for an escape from a fearful rout. Carlisle just went about its business.

They were still in the first quarter and again the Indians were in Harvard territory, down to the thirty-yard line. Again the advance stalled. Jim was still not running with the ball.

In the huddle the Indian quarterback turned to the Carlisle star.

"A kick will tie it up," he said.

"Give it to me," said Jim.

The ball came back from center. The whole Harvard

line converged on the Indian. Too late! From the forty-third-yard line the ball went end over end, straight through the Harvard uprights.

Score: Harvard 6, Carlisle 6.

The crowd raised a mighty shout. Little Carlisle was holding the great Johnny Harvard.

A slap on the back. "That was great, Jim!" And the Indian team moved stolidly back into position. Second team or first team, they were carrying the ball. This time it was from the thirty-seven-yard stripe. The center whipped the ball back to the great Thorpe; out went the toe, up went the ball, straight as a die for the mark. Percy Haughton wasn't smiling. Carlisle was leading 9 to 6, and the whistle ended the half.

In the locker room Haughton gave it to the Crimson squad straight from the shoulder. They were madder than hornets when they hit the field. They ripped they smacked, they rushed and they bulled their way through the Carlisle line. And their drive carried straight to the Indian goal line and over for the second Harvard score of the afternoon. No small school squad was going to stop them. They didn't reckon with Thorpe.

"I'm running with the ball," announced Jim in the huddle.

The Carlisle boys didn't argue with him this time.

"Gangway!" he yelled. "Get out of my way!"

Taped legs and all, Jim was on the move.

"Give me that ball!"

They gave him the ball.

Through right tackle, through left guard, straight through center, forgetting his blocks, leaving them behind, Thorpe plowed into that Harvard line, tearing a hole, smashing the linemen who came up to meet him, straight-arming the secondardies. In no time at all he was at the gates of a touchdown for Carlisle.

"Atta boy, Jim!"

His teammates huddled around him.

Haughton called time. Off the field came a bruised Harvard. Into the game went every best man on its eleven, every best man to stop that mad Indian.

It didn't work. Charge and rush, rush and charge, the great halfback carried the ball seventy yards down the field for six points to tie up the game again between little Carlisle and the highly touted team from Cambridge.

The twenty-five thousand fans were hoarse with shouting. They were witnessing a small miracle. As plain as day, Harvard was going to bow to the Indian school if they didn't stop Jim Thorpe.

They tried hard enough. Some of the boys from cultured Harvard tried so hard that they forgot their manners. One of the boys was thrown out for slugging. The others did their slugging when the referee wasn't looking. It was all the same to Jim. They carried the Cambridge boys off the field, too worn to move, but the Indian was up on his feet after every line buck, every savage block, every vicious tackle.

"This is fun," he said, helping a Cantab up to his squad. The tougher the fight the better he liked it. "Let's go!" he yelled.

The fourth quarter of the mighty duel found both teams pretty well spent. Still the battle kept its pace. Up and down the field they went, putting everything they had in each charge, each block, but neither team could strike pay dirt.

There were only minutes left to play. The exhausted crowd was ready to settle for a tie and a moral victory for the Indians. Not Jim Thorpe.

The ball was on the Cambridge forty-three-yard line but the Indians weren't going any farther with it.

"I'll boot it," said Jim.

"You've kicked three of them over."

"I'll boot it," said Jim.

"The odds are against it," argued the Carlisle squad.

"I'll boot it," insisted Thorpe.

The pass from center went to the great Indian. All Harvard knew he was going to try to kick it over. Every ounce of energy left in the squad rushed to stop it. They tore through the line, leaped high for the ball. They couldn't stop it. Jim Thorpe, standing just inside his fifty-yard stripe, got his toe on the pigskin—and up into the air it sailed, heading for the goal posts. Twenty-five thousand breathless spectators, every man on the field—Haughton, Warner, every football man in the park—stood up to watch the flight of that ball. End over end it went, spinning, tumbling, but straight and true as a beeline in its direction, and a thunderous shout shook the field as the ball shot between the two uprights guarding the Cambridge goal.

Score: Carlisle 18, Harvard 15.

They lined up for the kickoff again. The boys from Carlisle were determined to hold their slim lead, Cambridge steeled for the last great try. The boys from Harvard played like madmen, trying to pull victory out of defeat. Wendell, Fisher, Smith, Reynolds, Storer, one of the greatest squads to play for Johnny Harvard, gave everything they had. They smashed, they blocked, they ran with every ounce of stamina left in them, the will to win at fever pitch. For some of them this was the last game they would play for the Crimson. They gave those last minutes everything the toughest coach would demand, and more. It was the old college try at its height.

But it was not enough. The Indians had Jim Thorpe and there was no more scoring on that gridiron on that memorable day. Little Carlie had risen like a young David to upend, to humiliate the great Sampson which was Harvard. The name of Jim Thorpe had been written among the all-time greats of football, and everywhere, from one end of the country to the other, people spoke with amazement and pride of Thorpe's great feats.

"There's never been anything like him in football," they said, and there wasn't anyone, sports writer or just ordinary spectator, who would disagree.

Walter Camp, choosing his All-American eleven for 1911, listed Jim Thorpe as All-American halfback.

Football has never seen the equal of Jim Thorpe. Thirty-nine years have passed since that great season and football has yet to witness as great a runner, blocker, kicker, demon on the gridiron.

## nine

*I*N THE SPRING OF 1912 the greatest American athletes from every section of the country, North, South,
East and West, poured into the New York Giants' Polo
Grounds. The United States was selecting its top runners, hurdlers, high jumpers and field men to compete
in the greatest sport classic in the world, the spectacular, international, quadrennial Olympics.

Every four years, except when wars have intervened,
in the capital or some other great city of the country
fortunate enough to be chosen, a whole populace goes
all out to welcome the best-trained, the best-equipped
athletes in the world. They prepare an elegant stadium,
a gala welcome for the different representatives of the
invited countries; they deck out the city, then throng
to the arena to witness the greatest rivalries and the
toughest competition in the history of sport.

In 1912 the Olympics were to be held in Stockholm,

capital of Sweden, the neat little Scandanavian country
with its remarkably long list of great track and field
men. But it wasn't just Scandanavians the American
team would meet. There would be Englishmen,
Frenchmen, Russians, Australians, Germans, Italians,
men from all over the globe, men who were champions
in their own country and men with reputations which
had traveled beyond the borders of their homelands.
If a man was to carry home the laurels in Olympic
competition, he had to be more than good; he had to
be a world-beater.

But Americans love competition. The tougher the
pace the better they like it. There isn't a man who runs
or leaps or throws a javelin who wouldn't give anything just to compete in the Olympics.

Ralph Craig came from Detroit, Lippincott from
Philadelphia, Davenport from the University of Chicago and Duke Kahanamonka from Hawaii. Meredith
came from Mercenberg Academy and Jim Thorpe
from Carlisle. There wasn't a college, a club, a city,
a Y that didn't bend every effort to place a man on
the squad which was to represent the United States in
the great Stockholm Olympics.

In the high jump trials, Jim Thorpe cleared the bar
at a mere six feet five. This was one of the times Jim
really tried. He outjumped Alva Richards, the national
high jump champion, and was just five eights of an inch
short of the world record which was held at the time

by Mike Sweeney. The jump was enough, of course, to insure a spot for him on the Olympic team they were assembling at the Polo Grounds.

But there was something new being added to the Olympics this year.

"Only a man," argued the European coaches and track men, "who is an all-round athlete, an all-round competitor, is deserving of the title, World Champion."

The United States agreed.

"Let us revive the pentathlon and the decathlon," suggested the men from Europe.

The pentathlon is a five-event competition, the decathlon consists of ten events. Everyone knew that as far as stamina was concerned, and the ability of one man to compete in runs, hurdles and field events, the Scandanavian athletes had the edge. Everyone knew, too, that this was an attempt to stop the American domination of the world classic.

Still, no protest came from the United States. They just sat about, watched the competitors in the Giants' ball park and chose their men.

The Americans had a couple of good sprinters in Craig of Detroit, Meyer of New York City. Mel Sheppard was another great sprinter, and Lippincott and Davenport. For the pentathlon they had Menaul out of the University of Chicago. For the pentathlon and the decathlon, both, they had a pretty good prospect in Jim Thorpe, the Carlisle Indian. For the modern pentathlon, another new event for the Olympic classic, the United States had an army man, a young fellow called Patton, Lieutenant George Patton. It was this same Patton who was to be called "Blood and Guts" and who would lead his men, as a general, in a merciless drive against the Nazi supermen, and level them in World War II.

It was a good team of athletes that the United States had got together, and in the summer of 1912, to the accompaniment of bugle and drumbeat, with a wildly cheering send-off crowd that had assembled at the pier, they boarded a ship and set sail for Sweden, the land of the Vikings.

A sea voyage is generally the signal for rest and relaxation, but not for the Olympic squad from America. They laid out the broad jump mats, they set up the high jump bars, they measured off the sprints and ran around the deck. They were in the pink of condition when they said, "So long," to the Statue of Liberty. They were going to be in the pink of condition when they landed in Europe.

There was one exception. If Jim Thorpe took any practice jumps, nobody saw him. If Jim ran around the deck once, there was no witness. He was the most relaxed athlete aboard ship. He gave no sign of any pressure on him and couldn't understand why anyone should be tense about the Stockholm meet.

"Sure it's the Olympics," he said. "But it's fun, isn't it? What's all the sweating for?"

Craig, Lippincott and Davenport shook their heads

in wonder and continued their stints around the deck. They had heard about Jim's training habits. They had never quite believed them.

Certainly Jim didn't train the way a man who wins medals usually trains. He lounged in his steamer chair, found a hammock to swing in, looked out on the green water and the endless blue horizon. He liked to watch the big fish jumping over the surf.

"Look at that baby go!" he shouted, sitting up in his chair.

When the fish had gone back into the deep blue, Jim leaned back in his chair again. He didn't tell anybody else how to train. The likelihood, however, is that Jim put in a stretch or two at limbering up when nobody was looking. He could never possibly have established the record he did without tuning up his muscles at least once in a while. He just wasn't talking. As far as the rest of the team was concerned, Jim trained in a hammock.

In Stockholm it was more of the same.

One afternoon, however, shortly before the Olympic games got started, it looked as though Jim might be having a change of heart. He was lying in his hammock, thinking pleasant thoughts when, suddenly, his face turned serious, his eyes dark. Slowly he picked himself up. More slowly he walked to the sidewalk. He looked up and down the street. The street was empty. He took a piece of chalk from his pocket, made a mark on the sidewalk and then paced forward twenty-three feet. Here he made another mark. Johnny Hayes, the old Olympic marathon runner, was watching from his hotel, a big smile on his face. "The Indian," he said to himself, "is going to start training."

He was about to open his window and shout, "Hey! Jim! That looks like a pretty big piece of broad jump you've marked out for yourself. Do you think you can make it?"

But Johnny Hayes never opened that window. He watched the Indian survey the distance, as if it were something he had to memorize, then turn on his heels, walk back to his hammock, turn over on his side and go fast asleep.

Johnny Hayes had seen a lot of men train. He had watched Jim Thorpe throughout the sea voyage and shook his head disapprovingly. But this last piece of business was too much for him.

"Well," he said to himself, thoroughly thwarted, "I hope that Indian didn't strain himself too much, writing down those chalk marks," and he sank down into his chair, too exhausted from the experience to move.

But Jim did all right in that broad jump. He jogged up and down the field a couple of times, then said he was ready.

The United States coach looked at him, a little incredulously. He had seen Jim train.

"Ready for what?" asked the coach.

"Ready for the broad jump."

"Go ahead," said the coach, and it was only with

mild curiosity that he watched Jim Thorpe tear down the stretch to make his leap. He wasn't expecting much from him.

But the Carlisle Indian never lacked confidence in himself. He remembered the two chalk marks he had made on the sidewalk of Stockholm, remembered the distance between them, then leaped. Those chalk marks weren't accurate. They weren't accurate by two and seven-tenths inches. All Jim Thorpe did in that Olympic broad jump was to leap twenty-three feet two and seven-tenths inches. It was good enough, however, to win first place in the event for the United States. The broad jump was the first competition of athletes from all over the world in the new Olympic Pentathlon —and the American Indian had won it.

The next event in the pentathlon was the two-hundred-meter hurdles. Jim looked for his special hurdling shoes.

"I just left them here," he complained to Coach Warner.

"No one is going to walk away with your shoes," snapped back the coach. He was angry. He figured that Jim, in his usual easy way, had just forgotten to bring them along.

"Anybody seen my shoes?" yelled Jim.

Nobody had seen Jim's shoes.

"I just put them down before I did the broad jump," Jim tried to explain.

"That's great," said Warner. "We'll just run down to Spalding's and get you another pair."

"You didn't expect me to jump with them, did you?" asked Thorpe, a little annoyed.

Pop was too angry to answer, but Jim never stayed annoyed too long.

"Maybe I should have jumped with them," he said. "I might have cleared the stadium."

But Pop Warner wasn't interested in what his wild Indian might have done had he carried his hurdling shoes. The hurdles had to be run and his prize protégé needed something to put on his feet. He ran around till he found an extra pair of spikes and a pair of sprinting shoes nobody was using. Hurdling shoes need spikes for the heels as well as for the toes. He hammered those heels spikes into the sprinting shoes and impatiently handed them to his runner.

"Here!" he said. "I hope you don't end by breaking your neck on them."

No manufacturer would have dared to send the shoes Jim Thorpe put on, even to a cellar club team. They were the kind of shoes a boy will bang up for himself just to play at the game of running hurdles. They certainly weren't shoes to wear in a race against the best hurdlers in the world. But Jim didn't complain. He never complained.

"They look pretty good to me," he said, grinning again.

Pop Warner may have been used to Jim's quirks. This was too much for him. He just turned on his heels and walked off.

Jim laughed. He never fussed and he couldn't understand fussing. He laughed and walked to the post.

With the squeezing of the trigger of the starting gun, Jim was off. Regulation shoes or an amateur imitation of them, it didn't matter. Jim was out in front at the first hurdle. And he kept going, gathering momentum, and he didn't stop till he cut the tape at the finish line. He was in first. His time was fifteen and six-tenths seconds. It was a great mark. It was to stand up for thirty-six years until Bob Mathias won the event in the Olympics held in London. It took thirty-six years and a great deal of new technical knowledge of the event to beat the time Jim Thorpe had set with a pair of shoes Glenn Warner had fixed up for him in the emergency.

"Did you try?" was all Pop Warner asked him when the race was over.

"I guess I tried a little," said Jim, and he grinned.

The pride of Carlisle had won the first two events of the Pentathlon. He didn't do so well in the third event, the javelin hurl. He tossed the rod 153' 2-19/20". Although that's a long way to hurl the javelin, it won only third place for the amazing Thorpe.

"You're slowing down," said Coach Warner.

"I'll win the next two," answered Thorpe.

"Do you think you can?" egged on the knowing coach.

Warner knew how to get at his great Indian.

"I know I can!" shot back Jim Thorpe, and he meant it.

He threw the discuss 116' 8-4/10" to give him first place in that event. In the 1500-meter race he cut the tape in 4 minutes 44.8 seconds to place first again, and to keep his promise to Coach Warner.

"Well?" he demanded of his straight-face mentor.

"Not bad," said Glenn Warner, simply. "How are you going to do in the decathlon?"

It was an astoundingly low score of seven points which Jim Thorpe had come in with for the five-event competition. It was better than twice as good as that of the runner-up F. R. Bie of Norway, who had come in second with fifteen points. Third man in the event was J. A. Menaul from the University of Chicago with twenty-eight points. The United States did well enough in the new event which was supposed to put the Americans at a disadvantage.

As a matter of record, the Americans did very well for themselves all around in the great classic at Stockholm that year. They made a clean sweep of the hundred-meter sprint, Ralph Craig coming in first, Meyer second and Lippincott third. They did it again in the eight eighty with Meredith setting an Olympic record, running the race in one minute fifty-one and nine-

tenths seconds. Behind him, second and third, came
Sheppard and Davenport. Jim Meredith was only a
nineteen-year-old boy at the time. As for the young
lieutenant, George Patton, all he did was to win fifth
place in the modern pentathlon, which included events
in fencing, shooting, swimming, riding and running
a four-thousand-meter race.

It was a great American team in the best tradition
of American sport, but the feats of Jim Thorpe were
those of a competitor beyond compare. He had been
remarkable in the pentathlon. It would be too much
to ask any man to duplicate the victory in the decathlon. That is, it would be too much to ask of any man
but Jim Thorpe.

In the pentathlon Jim had won four firsts. In the
decathlon he won four again. He was first in the high
hurdles, coming in at 15.6 seconds; first in the 1500-
meter run, coming in at 4:40.1; first again in the high
jump with a leap of 6'1-6/10"; and first in the shot-put
with a toss of 42'5-9/20". He placed third in the 100-
meter race, the discuss throw, the pole vault and the
broad jump. He was fourth in the 400-meter and the
javelin events.

Competing in ten such varied events against the best
men in the world is to take on a most grueling pace,
even for skilled and highly trained athletes. To compete in ten such events, after the five events of the
pentathlon, is enough to kill off the heartiest of men.
But not Jim Thorpe.

After setting the seemingly impossible score of 7 points in the pentathlon, the Indian had gone on to score an unbelievable 8,412.96 points out of a possible 10,000. And of course, he was high man again, first. The nearest man to him was Hugo Wieslander of Sweden. The great Swede had scored a very creditable 7,724 points. But he was almost 700 points behind the great Indian from Carlisle.

With 7 points in the pentathlon, 8,412.96 in the decathlon; this was an athletic feat that was never to be repeated.

Before the tremendous crowd of sport enthusiasts who had gathered from all corners of the world to witness the greatest athletes via against each other, King Gustav of Sweden summoned the grandson of the Indian warrior, Black Hawk, to the victory stand.

"For winning the decathlon . . ." said the King of all Sweden, and Jim took from his hands a bronze bust cast in the likeness of the monarch.

"For winning the pentathlon . . ." continued the king, and he handed the boy from Carlisle the prize awarded by the Czar of all the Russias, a silver Viking ship, studded with magnificent jewels.

A laurel wreath was handed King Gustav and he draped it over the shoulders of the triumphant athlete.

"Sir," said His Majesty, "you are the most wonderful athlete in the world."

The return of the American heroes to their native shores was all pomp and splendor. Jim's welcome home was one long string of magnificent celebrations. The American athletes had come back with first place in the Olympics. Jim Thorpe had come home with first place in the heart of every American man, woman and child.

Jim Thorpe is the highest type of citizen, said the President of the United States, Howard Taft.

In New York there was a huge parade to welcome the Indian who had shown the world that a native American was the greatest living athletic competitor. There was a parade and a meet in Philadelphia. More of the same in Boston. At Carlisle the school went wild, welcoming the return of its three heroes, Louis Tewanima winner of the mile and the two-mile races at the Olympics, their great coach, Pop Warner, and the incomparable, the darling of the nation, smiling, modest Jim Thorpe, grandson of Chief Black Hawk of the Fox and Sac Indians.

It was a memorable moment in the life of the great athlete

"We'll pay you seven hundred and fifty dollars to do a stage tour," came one offer.

"We'll pay you one thousand dollars a week," came a second.

"We'll pay you one thousand five hundred dollars." Jim turned them all down.

"They don't understand," he explained. "I just can't talk to people."

Jim should have been able to talk. He might have been able to avert the tragedy which followed so close on the triumphant and happy days of the summer of 1912.

## ten

WHEN THE 1912 FOOTBALL season got under way, the eyes of the nation turned to that little Indian school which had been built at the end of a trolley line out of the small town of Carlisle. The man who had proved himself the greatest athlete in the world was going to play his last year of college football. The Indian had already won his gridiron spurs. Walter Camp had named him All-America halfback in 1911. But that was before he had come home with more than fifty thousand dollars' worth of trophies from the Stockholm Olympics. That was before James E. Sullivan, United States Commissioner to the Olympic games, declared, "He is unquestionably the greatest athlete who ever lived. Not one of the strong men of history could have competed with him successfully. They had great strength, we may infer," the commissioner had continued in his statement to the press, "but they lacked his speed, his agility, his skill. A wonder, a marvel, is the only way to describe him."

All America was behind him. He was one top man, who like Joe Louis thirty-five years later, America wanted to see stay top man. They knew Carlisle didn't have the man power of the big college teams on their gridiron schedule. They knew Carlisle didn't have the linemen, the blocking backs of the other schools. Yet Jim Thorpe was the superman of 1912 and, team behind him or not, America expected the Indian to scale even the tall heights of glory he had set in the season of 1911 when, singlehanded, he had brought down the flag of the mighty Percy Haughton—and Harvard.

They were not disappointed.

In the Dickinson game Carlisle was being hard pressed. Dickinson wasn't supposed to be one of the tougher schools on the Indians' schedule but the small college was doing all right by itself. It hadn't scored but neither had Carlisle. As a matter of fact, the Indian school had been deep in its own territory most of the first quarter. The only thing that had kept Dickinson from scoring was the mighty booting of Jim Thorpe. Every time he got his toe on the pigskin it sailed sixty and seventy yards down the field. Sooner or later, Dickinson felt, there'd be a bad pass from center. They were ready to capitalize on the bad throw they were sure was coming up. It was a matter of the law of averages and they were going to make the most of it.

Carlisle was jammed against its own goal line. Little Dickinson was on its toes.

"Eighty-five . . . twenty-nine . . . sixty-two. . . ."

The center was being pressed. His pass would have to go beyond the last Carlisle stripe.

"Ninety-six . . . eighty-four. . . ."

Back went the ball, wild!

Jim Thorpe leaped for the pigskin. He couldn't reach it. All Dickinson broke through. This was the break they had been looking for. A touchdown now would break the back of the Carlisle offensive. The guards broke through, the ends skirted the line, the secondary came in. They were fast, too. But Jim Thorpe was faster.

Twenty yards behind his goal posts he scooped up the ball, tucked it under his arm and began to move back. He side-stepped a would-be tackler, straight-armed another. He was up to the goal line, a Dickinson back came at him. Jim stopped dead in his tracks, watched the boy swing into the hard turf. Then he was off again like a streak for the Dickinson end of the gridiron. Once in the clear, there was no one who could catch up with the great Indian. There was no one but a referee to greet him as he crossed the last chalk mark. It was one of the greatest exhibitions of broken-field running in the history of football. The bad pass had been the beginning of the end, not for Carlisle but for Dickinson. Carlisle went on from there to finish the job easily. Final score: Carlisle 35, Dickinson 0.

It was the same story, with variations, at Lehigh. Lehigh had one of the good teams in the country. It always sent a well-drilled squad into the game, a squad that was likely to turn in a win against any of the top-notch Ivy Leaguers. The Lehigh-Carlisle game was a tossup for a while. Then Lehigh began to throw its weight around. They had pushed the Indians back to the three-yard line but there the Indians held. Three downs and the boys from Lehigh couldn't move the ball an inch. On the fourth down Lehigh passed. It was the short, flat pass just over the scrimmage line. All season long the play had worked for the short gain for a first down, for the touchdown when they were close enough to the goal posts. It didn't work against Carlisle.

Pazetti was Lehigh's quarterback. He was good enough to make Camp's second All-American. He called the signals. The ball didn't come back; he grabbed it right out of the center's hands, ran back a few steps, turned and shot it, straight as an arrow toward the end standing just about five yards beyond the Carlisle goal line.

But the Lehigh end never touched the ball. Jim Thorpe was there first, and his big hands eagerly gathered in the pigskin.

Any ordinary player—most good players—would have touched that ball down for a touchback. It would have been the easiest thing to do, with eleven men from

Lehigh on his neck. It would have brought the ball back to Carlisle's twenty-yard marker, as well as stoping the touchdown.

But Jim Thorpe was not that kind of player. He had the ball and he was going to run with it, even if half the Lehigh eleven clung to his shirt.

He twisted, he turned, he shook off half a dozen Lehigh gridders. He straight-armed one, straight-armed another. He wasn't more than ten yards over his own goal line before he was in the open—while behind him was only the Lehigh quarterback, Pazetti.

Straight down the field went Thorpe, Pazetti on his tail. He wasn't one to cut across to the side lines. Although Pazetti was a fast man, the fastest man on Lehigh's squad, he wasn't nearly fast enough for Jim Thorpe. For a moment the Indian slowed down. He actually let Pazetti come within two yards of him. Then he waved his hand at the all-out Lehigh quarter, just in token of farewell, and moved off, leaving a thoroughly frustrated Pazetti far behind him.

It was one hundred and five yards for the touchdown, Carlisle trimming Lehigh by the neat score of 34-14, but Jim was to do better as the season grew older.

Against Syracuse, Carlisle had been stopped for a full half. It was raining and the field was all mud. Jim's trick of running around end with his blazing speed wasn't much good in the mire. Syracuse hadn't done any better, the score was tied at 0-0, but Glenn War-

ner was a mad coach when he pushed into the Indians'
dressing room between the halves.

"We're not going anywhere on those runs around
end!" he snapped. "If you want to win this game you'll
have to hit them through the middle!"

Welch, the smart little Carlisle quarterback, and
Arcasa, Jim Thorpe's running mate at halfback, stirred
uncomfortably on their benches.

"I thought I had a team out there on the field!"
hammered Glenn Warner. "There's more than one
way to pick up your yardage!" he hollered.

The boys dug their heads deeper into their shoulders.
Pop looked across the room to where his great star
lay stretched out in a corner, yawning.

Jim didn't like playing in the rain. Pop Warner
knew it.

"What's the fun in getting your clothes wet?" Jim
said once, and Jim really played the game only when
it was fun.

"Maybe I ought to put someone into the game who
isn't afraid to buck the line!" needled Warner.

Jim stirred in his corner.

"Maybe I can get someone who isn't scared to bang
through tackle, smash through center!"

"Aw," came the noise from the corner, "what's the
use of running through them when you can run around
them?"

"Run around them!" exploded Pop Warner. "Who's
running around them?"

He was looking straight at Jim now, and he was madder than a hornet. All season long he had been trying to get the Indian to buck the line. All season long Jim had been making a joke of the business, stealing the game with his long runs sweeping the ends. The little joke had gone too far. Pop Warner let go with both barrels.

"Call yourself a ballplayer, do you?" he slammed at his great halfback. "You're a sprinter, maybe! You can lazy around the field, boot a ball and run a mile, if no one is near you! Can you blast a hole through the line? Can you bang your way through a guard, cut through tackle, blast your way through center? When you can do that, I'll say I've got a man who can play halfback for me! Right now, you're nothing but a loafing, lazy hunk of flesh and bone in a football uniform!"

And Warner didn't let up on his star till Jim Thorpe's face was red and his fists were clenched with anger.

"All right," said Pop. "I've said my piece. Now go out on the field and hit the middle or take a licking. I'm not calling the signals and I'm not running with the ball. You are!"

The boys in the locker room were quiet. It wasn't often that Pop Warner let go the way he did. No one dared speak. No one dared even look at Jim Thorpe, still lying in his corner, smoldering. Syracuse paid for that little interlude.

The Indians came out on the run.

"Give me that ball!" Jim snapped at his quarterback. "Through left tackle!" he shouted across to the boys from Syracuse.

Welch called the signals. The ball was handed to Jim and through left tackle he went, driving, smashing, slashing like an avenging angel. There was no one in the Syracuse line who could stop him. There wasn't a man playing football that afternoon who could have stopped him in that second half. Glenn Warner knew it. He knew, too, how to get the great Indian moving.

That second half was unadulterated slaughter. Three times Jim went over the line for touchdowns. His fierce and merciless line plunging set up two more touchdowns, one by quarterback Welch, the other by Powell. The game ended with completely outclassed Syracuse at the short end of a 33-0 blanking.

"Can I play football for you?" demanded the Indian, coming back to the bench.

Pop said nothing, but when the gridder turned on his heels and walked off in a huff he allowed himself a well-earned small grin of satisfaction.

Lebanon was whitewashed 45-0. Georgetown scored twenty-four points but Carlisle scored thirty-four. Albright was swamped 50-7. Villanova was washed under 65-0. Springfield came close but Carlisle was on top 30-24.

"Thorpe will never run through us again," declared Colonel Joe Thompson of Pittsburgh to the press before game time. "We've got him figured out."

In that game Thorpe scored two touchdowns, kicked a field goal, six conversions and made a shambles of the colonel's team with his slashing long gains of twenty and thirty and forty yards. The Indian was smashing an amazing number of points against all opposition. Football talk was all Jim Thorpe, wherever people talked gridiron. Never in its history had the sport boasted such a competitor.

Army had one of the toughest teams in the East in 1912. Devore and Weyand were two All-American tackles, Merillat an All-American end and Prichard an All-American quarterback. They were waiting for Jim Thorpe the way the rest of the American gridders had waited for the powerful Indian.

"Break Thorpe's leg, break his arm," was the rumor that floated around every campus, "and you've won your letter."

Of course, no one was out to maim the ghost from Carlisle, but no one opposing him wanted to see the Indian maverick in the game any longer than he had to be. The battle cry was "Stop Thorpe! If we're going to win the game, stop Thorpe!" There wasn't a player who didn't know he'd be the hero of the college if he could knock the Indian off the gridiron.

But wishing . . . dreaming . . . hoping . . . are a long way from the real thing. It was one thing to say, "Stop Thorpe!" It was quite another thing to do it.

Thorpe looked over the cadets from West Point,

Devore, Weyand, Merillat and the others. He knew they were "laying" for him. Weyand was playing guard that day. They had a two-hundred-pounder by the name of Red O'Hare playing tackle with Devore. Jim wasn't impressed.

"All right, boys," he said, "let's show the Army what the Indians can do."

Maybe Jim was thinking of the long series of defeats his Indian ancestors had tasted at the hands of the United States Regulars. Maybe he was thinking of the humiliation of his grandfather, Chief Black Hawk of the Fox and Sac. If he did, it was entirely without malice. It was just football to Jim, and football was fun.

"Through tackle!" yelled Jim.

Welch, Carlisle's gritty quarterback called the numbers. The ball was snapped back to Thorpe, and through tackle, as advertised, went the smashing Indian.

Red O'Hare was waiting for him. He nailed him with all the bulk of his two hundred pounds. That is, he hit him with two hundred pounds.

Any ordinary gridder would have been dropped like a ton of bricks, stopped dead in his tracks. But Jim Thorpe was no ordinary gridder.

"When I came to," said Red O'Hare, after the game, "I was across the side lines, at the edge of the stands. I don't know how I got there, but there I was. I thought a cyclone had struck."

It wasn't a cyclone, or a tornado either. It was Jim
Thorpe. The Indian was too much for the best of West
Point, with all the All-Americans on its squad.

Early in the first quarter Jim carried three Army men
and the pigskin over the goal line for Carlisle's first
score. For a change of pace, with the whole Cadet
Corps coming his way, Jim tossed passes to his running
mate for another score. When he wasn't running or
passing he was keeping Army deep in its own territory
with his phenomenal boots, which averaged over sixty
yards during the whole long afternoon.

At one point in the game Jim got tired of kicking
the pigskin. It was fourth down and the Indians had
the ball on their own ten-yard line. Everybody, including the boys on the Carlisle squad, knew that the
next play called for one of Thorpe's long boots.

Welch barked off the signals. The ball went back
to Jim and Jim faded back to punt. With him went the
late Bill Langford, who was refereeing the game.

"They think I'm going to kick," said Thorpe to the
astounded referee, while half of the Army team was
closing in on the Indian. "But I ain't!" declared Jim.

He faked the punt, all right, then stuck the ball under
his arm and started to run. Only a man who played the
game for fun would have pulled a stunt like that, and
Jim, of course, played for fun.

Army, however, didn't think it was funny at all.
They plowed into him, hit him with everything they
had—Devore, Merillat, Weyand, O'Hare and a young

fellow called Ike Eisenhower. But the whole Army team wasn't enough to cut down that run, and Jim Thorpe didn't stop till he had scored another touchdown for little Carlisle. He had everyone—including Welch, Powell, Arcasa and even Pop Warner—fooled on that play.

In the second half Jim pulled another stunt, and this one put the lid on Army for the rest of the day.

Army had the ball. They were kicking off after another Carlisle touchdown. It was a good kick. It went all the way to the Indian ten-yard marker. Unfortunately for West Point, however, it was Jim Thorpe who picked up the pigskin, forgot his blockers, and ran through all the cadets for another score.

Jim handed the ball to the referee and started back to his lines, ready to run back another kickoff, but the referee, instead of indicating the touchdown, called the play back.

"No good!" he said. "No good!"

Jim just looked at him.

"Off side!" pointed the referee, indicating the Carlisle squad. "Off side."

The West Point rooters were too numb to yell their approval. The Indians shrugged their shoulders and went back into position. Jim had done it once, he could do it again.

Army booted. Ths time the ball hit the five-yard stripe. Again Thorpe scooped it up, this time on the run. He weaved, bobbed, struck out his good right arm. Cadets fell all over the field, following their brief encounter with the granite man from Carlisle, and it took little more than a sprint for the Indian for a ninety-five-yard touchdown.

"It counts this time, doesn't it?" he asked the referee, still holding the pigskin.

"Touchdown!" snapped the arbiter.

Jim walked back across the field, while the stands at West Point shook like thunder.

"That's the longest run I've ever made," said Jim to his teammates, "for one lonely touchdown. One hundred and eighty-five yards, if I count it right."

"Right," said Welch, slapping Thorpe's broad back.

"Right," said Arcasa, with a grin as big as Jim's.

They never could get close to Thorpe. Jim just wouldn't open up for anybody. But all Carlisle was mighty proud of him.

While it may not have been with pride, it was with the utmost respect that his opponents regarded the giant among the football men.

"That Indian," said Devore, captain of the Army team, when the West Point eleven got back to its lockers, "is the greatest player I ever saw in my five years of experience." Devore was no slouch himself. He stood six feet four, was the best tackle in the country and perhaps the strongest man in football. But his respect for Thorpe was second to none. "That man," he said, talking to the press, "is superhuman, that's all. There is no stopping him.

"Talk of your Ted Coys," continued the amazed Army captain, "why, this Indian is as far ahead of Yale's great back as Coy was better than a prep school player. There is nothing he cannot do. He hits the line about twice as hard as Coy did. He kicks better in every respect, and he is far more cunning and capable of worming his way through a scattered field. There never was a man who knew more about following interference and breaking away from it at just the proper moment to his best advantage."

Devore wasn't finished.

"You may have your Lefty Flynns and your Brickleys and your Ted Coys," he added, naming the legendary gridders of his time, "but I'll take Thorpe for mine every day in the week."

Everybody in football said, "Amen."

The admiration and adulation was enough to turn anyone's head. Not Jim's. He took it all as a matter of course.

Thorpe scored twenty-two points that afternoon. The final score of the game: Carlisle 27, Army 6.

Brown was the last game on the 1912 Carlisle gridiron schedule, and the last college football game for Jim. Brown, of Providence, Rhode Island, in the year 1912, boasted an All-American quarterback, Crowther. Purdy, its substitute quarterback, made Walter Camp's second team on the All-America. Kulp at guard was on the second All-America, too. It was a good, strong team and promised to give Carlisle plenty of fight.

The game was played in a snowstorm, the kind of weather that was calculated to slow up Jim Thorpe. Brown's hopes were high when their All-American Crowther led them onto the gridiron. The hopes didn't last too long.

Playing his last football for little Carlisle Jim put in a magnificent performance. Three times he ran fifty yards and more to score three touchdowns for Carlisle and Pop Warner. Seconds before the final whistle, he tossed a twenty-five-yard pass to Wheelock and then slammed through the entire Brown defense to score his last points for the great little Indian school which had helped build him into America's greatest athlete.

There was no question about Jim's place on the All-American team. For the second time in two years Walter Camp placed him at halfback for the first team. The greatest football player Devore of Army had seen —anyone else had seen—had scored twenty-five touchdowns and one hundred and ninety-eight points in the single season of 1912, a record no player on any of the major college elevens has ever approached.

Jim Thorpe had made school football history. He bowed out of college football in a blaze of glory.

## eleven

AT THE END OF 1912 Jim Thorpe was sitting pretty. The greatest gridder the country had ever seen, champion of the United States Olympic team, recognized all over the world as an athlete beyond compare, he was the uncrowned king of sports, every sport on the calendar. The football season hadn't ended before five of the big-league baseball teams came down to little Carlisle to bid for the mighty Indian. The winter of 1912 was cold. The winds roared and the snows piled up during the last days of the dying year, but the days were full of sunshine for James Francis Thorpe, and full of hope. His mother had named him Bright Path, after the gleam of the sun which poured into the window of her little cabin. The road that Jim, grandson of Chief Black Hawk's, seemed destined to travel glittered with promise.

And then, almost without warning, the sunny skies which had seemed to move wherever Jim moved became clouded over. A noise more ominous than the wind and more destructive than thunder began to come in from the East. At first it was no more than a rumor. Then the storm broke, torrents of abuse came tumbling down on the head of the great warrior and, almost overnight, he was toppled from his throne.

There are many versions of the story. Jim says it was a former pitcher, who had become a newspaper sports writer, who turned the trick. The pitcher had played ball for the Fayetteville ball club in North Carolina the year Jim had been on its roster, and late in 1912 had recognized the Indian on a picture the team had taken on a hunt. It was a snapshot Clancy the manager of the ball club had taken, blown up and hung on a wall in his ranch house. Jim was riding a mule, but the mule was no disguise. The sports writer recognized him, and early in January, 1913, he wrote for the Worcester, Massachusetts, paper that hired him:

"Jim Thorpe played professional baseball in 1909-10 for Rocky Mount and Fayetteville in the Eastern Carolina League."

Another version of the story has Francis Albertanti, a rookie sports reporter, as the man who broke the news which rocked the sports world.

Albertanti was working for the New York *Evening Mail*, which has since gone out of existence. He was also editing an amateur sports sheet. As a matter of fact, amauteur sports were his specialty and the big games were covered by the paper's two top-notch sports writers. One was Franklin P. Adams, more famous later on for his column in the New York *World* and for his humor as a newspaperman and a member of the permanent squad of Information Please experts. The other great sports writer with the *Evening Mail* was the now-venerable sports authority, Grantland Rice.

As far as F.P.A. and Rice were concerned, there was no blemish on the amateur record of the great Thorpe. Albertanti, himself, had no advance knowledge of the professional activities of the great Indian. He was sitting in the office, mulling over some old newspaper clippings and some of the out-of-town magazines which had floated in.

"Say! Look at this!" he shouted suddenly, above the noise of the clattering typewriters.

Nobody looked. Everybody was too busy with his own story. Albertanti jumped up from his chair and shoved the clipping under the nose of Grantland Rice.

"Read this!" he demanded.

Grantland Rice looked up at the young reporter, read the clipping, turned back to the cub and said nothing.

"What do we do with it?" asked the excited Albertanti. "What do we do?"

"What do you want to do with it?"

"Give it to Kirby!" Kirby was president of the A.A.U. "Give it to Sullivan!" Sullivan was its secretary.

Rice just handed the clipping back to the young reporter.

"I guess they'll want to see it," said Albertanti.

He wasn't sure himself.

"I suppose so," said Rice, and he turned back to his typewriter.

Whichever way the Amateur Athletic Union learned of Jim's playing with the Eastern Carolina League the result was the same. Sullivan got in touch with Coach Warner and Warner called in Thorpe.

There was no beating around the bush.

"You played ball when you weren't at Carlisle?" said Pop Warner.

"I told you that when I came back," said Jim, still completely unaware of what was in store for him.

"Baseball?" continued Pop Warner.

"Sure. I played for Rocky Mount and Fayetteville and. . . ."

"Did you get paid for it?"

"Sure, I got paid for it," said Jim. "Everybody got paid for it."

"Don't you know an amateur isn't supposed to play for money?" exploded Pop.

He got up from his chair and began to pace the room. Pacing the room was Jim's trick, but the truth had suddenly dawned on the Indian and he was too stunned to move.

"But everybody plays ball and gets paid for it, Pop," he protested.

"And gives his right name, too?" snapped the coach. "You sure have handed yourself a mess! How do you expect to pull out of it?"

"I didn't know I was doing anything wrong," said Jim, simply. "I hope this doesn't give you any trouble, Coach."

"Me!" bellowed Warner. "Don't you worry about me! It's all those medals you brought back from the Olympics. It's the king's head and that Viking ship they want!"

Thorpe was thoroughly beaten. He didn't understand. During July and August the roster of every semipro club was jammed with college football and baseball players. True, they played under some assumed name, but Jim didn't see that that made any difference. They must have known that he had played semipro ball. There were big-league scouts who had come down to watch him play. Everybody knew that Jim Thorpe had pitched for Rocky Mount, he figured. Why did they wait till now to make a fuss about it?

"It's too much for me to make out," he said, quietly. "I sure would hate to give up those trophies," he added in a voice which didn't carry to the other end of the room.

Pop Warner put his hand on the Indian's shoulder.

"We've got to do something about it," he said. "The A.A.U. wants to talk to us."

The proud Indian, like his ancestors before him, was forced to lower his colors. He had played ball for a bush club in a bush league, never earned more than sixty dollars a month doing it. That, by itself, hadn't created even a ripple in the big ocean of the sports world. But his name had appeared in the line-up of the club. It was as Jim Thorpe that he had pitched or played in the infield or patrolled the garden. He had been too honest, or too simple. All the other boys who had earned the "honest dollar" during their vacations had been smart enough to take on another name, such as Joe Smith, Bill Brown, John Doe. But not Jim Thorpe. That name Jim Thorpe in the Fayetteville roster was enough to whip up as fierce a storm as the ocean of athletics had ever witnessed.

"I did not play for the money that was in it," Jim wrote to the moguls of the Amateur Athletic Union, "but because I like to play ball."

Everybody in the game—football, baseball, track, basketball, lacrosse—knew that Jim only played for the fun of it.

"How many events do you want to get into?" Coach Murphy of the United States Olympic squad had asked the Indian.

"All of them," Jim had answered. "What's the fun of watching when you can play?"

This was Jim Thorpe. He was always an amateur at heart, the greatest of the amateurs, and he never changed. He was first, last and always a competitor. That fifteen dollars a week would never make him rich, but he got a kick out of swinging a bat, fielding a hot grounder, whipping the old apple down the middle, making it dance around the plate, slamming it past the swinging batter for a *K* in the score book.

"I did not play for the money," Jim wrote. However, it was that money and his name—the fifteen dollars a week to an Indian named Bright Path and called Jim Thorpe—which had upended the equilibrium of the great amateur world of sports and threatened to send all the trophies won by a magnificent athlete back to Sweden.

"I was not very wise in the ways of the world," continued the humbled Thorpe in his letter to James E. Sullivan, secretary of the A.A.U., "and did not realize that this was wrong."

The big leagues knew that Jim had played semipro ball. There must have been a lot of others who knew that Jim had played in the bush league. The Indian certainly wasn't "wise in the ways of the world" which let him compete in the trials for the Olympic team, allowed him to go abroad with the United States squad, allowed him to receive the plaudits of a king and a czar and accept their magnificent trophies, only to reverse itself and blacken and besmirch his name.

They must have known, thought Jim, and they said nothing until the newspapers blew the thing up into an issue.

But the Indian people are a stoic people. They can

be humble in all their pride, accept punishment without complaining, suffer great pain, even death, without uttering a cry in protest.

"I hope I will be partly excused by the fact that I was simply an Indian school boy and did not know that I was doing wrong," he wrote in all simplicity and sincerity, "because I was doing what many other college men had done, except they did not use their own names."

Jim Thorpe was simple enough to speak the plain truth, but college men playing professional ball under assumed names had ever been a source of irritation to the simon-purists of athletics. They might forgive Jim his errors, taking into consideration his great humility. They could never forgive his bringing into the open again the semipro excursions of college and school athletes.

"If Thorpe is guilty," declared James Sullivan on the eve of the meeting of the A.A.U., the meeting to decide the fate of the Indian, "we want to find it out as soon as possible. We have no desire to cover up the doings of anyone connected with the A.A.U. who may be charged with having broken the laws of amateur competition. This is a matter in which a delay is dangerous to the best interests of the union, and because of Thorpe's chances to be accredited greatest athlete in America is no reason why prompt action should not be taken."

The Amateur Athletic Union was on the spot. Jim Sullivan was really one of Thorpe's great admirers.

"It has been said," he told the press, "that sustained charges against Thorpe would not be acted upon with the speed that would prevail in the case of an ordinary athlete. In reply to this I will say that we will act with greater dispatch than would prevail with the action in regard to any other athlete in America."

There was more than Jim Thorpe at stake as far as the A.A.U. was concerned. There was its honor in accepting the Olympic championship with a man who might not be simon-pure.

"While it has never been shown that he has broken the amateur law in any form of track and field competition," explained the secretary, "the fact that he signed a registration blank attesting that he had never in any manner transgressed the amateur rule makes him amenable to discipline by the Amateur Athletic Union."

Sullivan then took a crack at organized baseball.

"The remarkable feature of the case," he said bitterly, "is that the baseball sharps of the country have not intimated this reputed wrongdoing long before this. It is known that the Pittsburgh League team managers had their eyes on Thorpe several years ago, and yet aside from rumors that Thorpe was slated to join that team nothing else was known of his alleged professional tendencies until last week."

But, whatever the guilt of others involved in the case

of Jim Thorpe, however innocently he committed a fault, the A.A.U. would adamantly uphold its principles of amateur athletics.

"If he is found to have broken the rules," said Mr. Sullivan severely, "he will be stripped of all his records; his name taken from the athletic annuals, and he will be compelled to return all the prizes he has won since his infraction of the rules."

It was a sharp note. The next day the Amateur Athletic Union voted Jim Thorpe "Guilty."

The reaction of the everyday American, the American who loves a champion but will more often cheer his throat hoarse for the underdog, was an instant and noisy anger.

"Who's the A.A.U.?"

"Who's this Kirby? Who's Sullivan?"

"What right have they got to take Thorpe's medals from the greatest athlete this country ever had?"

There were some few who applauded the action of the A.A.U., and Jim came in for some bad name-calling. But fans from the Atlantic to the Pacific, from Maine to Palm Beach, called it a shame, a hypocritical shame. Jim Thorpe, the "loner," the man with millions of admirers, was discovering for the first time that he had friends, too.

According to Damon Runyon, one of America's great sport writers:

"It seems a little enough thing that this great Carlisle star did. . . . Today this league [Eastern Carolina League for which Jim played], probably never very hale and hearty in its most prosperous days, is defunct, but it lived long enough to furnish a means of destruction for the career as an amateur of the greatest athlete of all times."

As if this weren't enough, Runyon added, "It develops that down south where Thorpe played, and among his friends and associates, there was no secret of the fact that he played baseball for money—they did not know that there was any particular harm in it. During the Olympic games, southern papers printed stories and pictures of the great Indian, lauding his prowess and constantly referring to his baseball connections in the Carolinas, and no hint of this reached the ears of the A.A.U. authorities."

Here was condemnation of the source of Jim's evil days put as nakedly and undeniably as possible. The A.A.U. did not answer.

Jim was heartened by his support, overwhelmed by all the evidence of friendship around him, but he took the verdict as delivered in true Indian style, in true Jim Thorpe style. He left the returning of his Olympic trophies to Pop Warner and not until years later did he ever make any comment on an action he could not possibly accept in his heart as just. He deserved better treatment from his white brethren.

Pop Warner wrapped up the sculptured head of the King of all Sweden. He wrapped up the Viking ship which the Czar of all the Russians had awarded his great Indian. He wrapped up all Jim's medals and ribbons. With a heavy heart he sent them back to Sweden.

Norway's F. R. Bie was declared the winner of the pentathlon. He was offered the sculptured replica of the head of his monarch which Jim had been forced to return. But the Norwegian would have none of it.

"Thorpe won the pentathlon," he said, simply. "The head belongs to him."

To Sweden and H. Wieslander, who was declared the winner of the Olympic decathlon, went the Viking ship.

"Not for me," said the great Swedish athlete. "I did not win the decathlon. The greatest athlete in the world is Jim Thorpe."

Jim never did get back those trophies. They are kept in a case and displayed, permanently, in the little neutral country of Switzerland. No one can find the great, unmatched record of Jim Thorpe's Olympic feats in any official record book, but anybody who wants to can travel to Lucerne in the Alps to see the great trophies he won but could not keep.

## twelve

$J$IM THORPE WAS DOWN but he was far from out. It would take more than a decision by the Amateur Athletic Union to retire the driving Indian. He may have lost his mythical crown that went with his being the monarch of all amateur sports, but he was much too great an athlete to be put on the shelf for any length of time.

In New York, in the offices of the National League Champions of 1911 and 1912, the tough Little Napoleon of baseball, John McGraw, manager of the Giants, had a hunch.

"How about this Indian?"

He was speaking to Foster, secretary of the club.

Foster knew how McGraw felt about college and school ball players.

"I don't like them! I don't want any part of them!"

It was inviting a withering blast from a champion tongue whipper to mention a college athlete to the toughest manager in the baseball business.

"You mean Thorpe?" said Foster, quietly. "Jim Thorpe from Carlisle?" he added.

"I hear he's a pretty good ballplayer," said McGraw, paying no attention to the secretary of the New York Club.

"He can run," offered Foster, tentatively.

"You've got to get on base before you can run them!" snapped the Little Napoleon.

"That's right," agreed Foster, who was quite ready to agree with the tempestuous manager. "I hear there are a couple of clubs after him."

"Is that so?" asked McGraw, as if he didn't know. "Did you read these reports? Seems the scouts all like him."

"They say he's got a pretty good arm," suggested Foster.

"For the bush leaguers!" shot McGraw who couldn't quite forget that Jim had come up from a school and not off the sandlots or out of some triple A club. "They're all nine-day wonders in the bushes!" added the blunt manager, as if he were trying to convince himself.

Foster turned back to the papers on his desk.

"Why don't you forget him?" he said.

McGraw didn't answer for a minute. He walked over to the window, paced up and down the room, stopped in front of Foster's desk.

"Get Glenn Warner for me. Call him. If this Indian can hit in batting practice it'll be enough for me."

Foster picked up the telephone, looked up at the manager.

"What are you waiting for?" spit the angry Little Napoleon. "He'll pull enough people to the park to pay for his contract. He's a drawing card."

"Just about the best drawing card in the country," said Foster, and he got Pop Warner on the phone.

"I hear that you've got a ballplayer down in Carlisle with you."

It was a different McGraw, soft spoken, almost indifferent, but Pop Warner was an old hand at this sort of game.

"I've got a couple of them, John," he said. "Who do you mean?"

"The Indian," said McGraw, still playing the part.

"They're all Indians," came back Warner, patiently.

John McGraw didn't like being bested in any deal, especially in a deal with a college coach.

"Call them off," he snapped.

And Warner called them off, a dozen of them before he called out Jim Thorpe.

"He's the Olympic man, isn't he?" asked McGraw, giving it no special emphasis. "He played ball, semipro ball in some Eastern Carolina League, I hear."

"You heard right," said Pop.

"How did he do with the bush league?" asked the manager, still pretending only the slightest interest in the man.

"Look here," came back the Carlisle coach. "I know

you called to get the low-down on the boy and I'll give to to you straight."

"That's the way I like it," came back the hard-boiled manager.

"All right," said Warner. "He just isn't fair, the way you put it. He's great! He's the world's best! And if you want him for your club, you'll have to out-bid every team in the National and American League both!"

"Get the Indian and put him on the phone!"

That was the way the Little Napoleon of baseball did business.

"I hear from the boys who scouted you," he said to Jim, "that you're a pretty good prospect."

Jim didn't answer. He was never much on the social amenities.

"I'd like you to come up with the Giants," Mac went on. "It's a tough, fighting, running, hot team. It's the kind of team you ought to play with. It's the kind of ball club that can use a player like you."

"How much are you going to pay me?" asked Jim, and Pop Warner, listening, smiled.

Jim wasn't much good on figures, but he knew enough to ask how much.

"I'll give you forty-five hundred a season on a three-year contract," McGraw offered.

Forty-five hundred a year was a lot of money for Jim Thorpe. Forty-five hundred was a lot of money for anybody in those days. It was a salary only the top men in baseball drew at that time, and there were very few who even dreamed of getting it.

But Jim wasn't familiar enough with numbers to be impressed.

"That's what they've all been offering," he said.

"I'll make it five thousand!" shot back McGraw.

Jim looked at Pop. He covered the mouthpiece of the phone with his hand.

"He's offering me five thousand and a three-year contract. What'll I tell him?"

"Tell him you'll call Friday. Tell him you want to think it over."

"I'll call you back Friday," reported Jim, like the schoolboy he was. "I want to think it over."

The Chicago White Sox had bid for Thorpe, the St. Louis Browns, the Cincinnati Reds and the Pittsburgh Pirates. Two of the clubs had sent scouts and the scouts had spent a whole week in Carlisle, trying to sign him up. But the pennant-winning Giants with the immortal Christy Mathewson, Tesreau, Heinie Groh, Doyle, George Burns and the rest of the fighting club was the glamour team in baseball. It promised the most action, the most excitement, to the game-loving Thorpe.

"That's the team for me," he said to Coach Warner, and Warner nodded his head and said, "That's the team for you, Jim, but McGraw is a tougher man than I'll ever be. You'll have to work. You'll have to work hard."

Jim looked at his coach. He could never understand how anybody thought of a ball game as work. It was fun. It was always fun or else it wasn't worth the effort a man put into it.

"I like to play the game," he said.

"That's half of it, Jim," said Pop Warner, trying hard to impress the Indian with the fact that professional ball playing meant a lot of sweating, a lot of training, and always sticking to the rules which make a good athlete. "The rest of it, Jim," he said, "is the grind, keeping yourself in condition. You've got to keep yourself in condition, good condition."

Jim was puzzled.

"But I'm always in good condition, Pop," he protested.

Warner shrugged his shoulders. There was no sense pressing the point. Jim Thorpe would never be the ideal athlete as far as training was concerned.

"All right, Jim," he said. "I know you'll make it. Good luck."

The Indian looked at the poker-faced, straw-chewing coach. Pop Warner had come in for a lot of criticism on his account, undeserved criticism. There were some who said that Warner should have known about the summers Thorpe played ball in Carolina, and that he should have stopped the Indian before he even tried out for the Olympic team. Jim knew how much Pop had taken and how Pop had stuck by him throughout the ordeal. But Jim could never find the words to tell

the great coach how he felt about him, how much he
had meant to him in all his years at Carlisle.

"Good luck," said Pop Warner—and all Jim could
say was, "Thanks."

On Friday he called New York.

"I'll take that five thousand," he said to McGraw.

"Good!" said the manager.

"That's for three seasons?" said Jim.

"Three seasons," repeated Mac. "Five thousand each
season."

"Fine," said Thorpe, and then he let go with what
was a long speech for a man who could never address
even the hero-worshipers who came to greet him on his
triumphant return from the Stockholm Olympics.

"You've got a great club, Mr. McGraw," he said,
"and I'm happy to sign up with a great club like the
New York Giants."

McGraw wasn't so sure. All his doubts about college
athletes began to trouble him again. He wasn't certain
that he hadn't made a mistake. Jim was going to give
him a lot of trouble. But the trouble wasn't going to
be about his hitting or his running or his throwing, and
it wasn't going to be because Jim was coming from
some sacred cathedral of learning. His great trouble
with Jim would arise from the clash of personalities.
They were two tough, fighting, headstrong men, both
John McGraw and Jim Thorpe. When two strong
men meet and one tries to tame the other, there is always trouble. There was no exception to the rule when

the Sac and Fox Jim Thorpe landed in the dugout of the New York Giants and came face to face with the mightiest warrior in baseball, the hardheaded, quick tempered, man-eating John McGraw.

## thirteen

*J*IM REPORTED FOR spring training with the New
York Giants at Marlin Springs, Texas early in 1913.
The camp was jammed with some of the greatest names
in baseball. The Giants had been top team in the National League for two years running, and the experts
were already predicting McGraw's men were going to
make it three championships in a row. Any other
young fellow walking into the New York clubhouse
might have been excused if his tongue got tied up and
his knees wabbled a little bit. Not Jim Thorpe. He
picked up his uniform, read the big letters spelling
GIANTS across his shirt and began to dress without a
change of pace.

Christy Mathewson, Heinie Groh, George Burns,
Doyle, Demaree, all big names in the national game,
watched the Indian get into his togs. They had read
a lot about him, heard a lot about him, but this was
their first look at the man who had carted away all
the big prizes from the Stockholm Olympics.

"I'm Mathewson."

The big pitcher offered his hand and Jim took it firmly.

"I'm glad you're on my team," said the Indian, and the whole clubhouse loosened up.

"Heinie Groh."

"Damaree. That's me."

It was give and take. Each man in the room had earned himself a niche in the world of sports. Each man was respected for the way he played the game. There was no need for anyone to kowtow to anyone else. They were all equals in the Giant clubhouse. It was the equality and fraternity which had helped mold them into a championship team. It was an equality and fraternity which Thorpe always wanted. He would accept nothing less. But there was something else about the Giants that Jim liked.

In 1913 baseball was a good deal rougher and tougher than it is today. Fights came a dime a dozen and there wasn't a man in a baseball uniform who wasn't quicker with his fists than he was with words. They didn't have the extensive farm systems we have now, gradually bringing up a player till he is just right for big-league ball. They didn't go in for hitting machines and pitching machines in spring training camp. Nor was discipline among the players the curfew kind of discipline we have today. Nobody thought of curbing the boys from betting on horse racing, playing cards and drinking. There was plenty of hard drinking those days, yet except when it interferred too much with the club no one said very much about it. As long as a man got down to the park in time, and did a good stint on the diamond, that was all that was expected of him. Without doubt, there are still ballplayers who get out of line occasionally, even today, but not for long. Today a big-leaguer can't even take a day off on the golf links without getting a good bawling out. Baseball is still a tough game and requires all the stamina and vigor a man can give it, but baseball today is a gentleman's game compared with the spike-flying, fist-flying game of 1913.

And there was no rougher, tougher bunch of men in either league that could compare with the fighting men of John J. McGraw's. John J., himself, was one of the toughest men on the diamond. He had to be to hold his big Giants in order.

"I don't like this horsing around!" snapped the Little Napoleon.

Jim had gotten right into the spirit of the hustling camp of New York's big team. He had been tussling with Jeff Tesreau.

"Get out onto that field and loosen up!"

Tesreau was a scrapper without equal but he knew better than to cross John J.

"O.K.," he said, picked up his glove and began to move into the field.

Not Jim Thorpe.

He looked the little manager up and down.

"I'm loose," he said. He flexed his muscles. "See. I'm loose."

"Get out onto that field!" snapped McGraw.

Jeff tugged on Jim's arm.

"Let's go, Jim."

Jim took a last look at the Little Napoleon and picked up his glove.

"You can't talk back to John," cautioned Jeff. "He doesn't like it."

"I don't like being pushed around," countered Thorpe.

Tesreau shrugged his shoulders. There was trouble coming.

McGraw watched the Indian in the field. Jim hadn't had any real coaching in baseball but he caught on fast. John J. watched him chasing a fly, catching it. He had never seen anyone as fast in a ball park. He watched him snap the ball on a line to the catcher from deep in center field and he had never seen a ball thrown so hard.

"He looks like a pretty good boy," said Christy Mathewson.

"Terrific!" said the Little Napoleon.

But when the Indian came in from the field the tough manager wasn't handing out any bouquets.

"Let's see you hit!" he ordered.

Jim got into the batting cage. The first ball was low

He let it go. The next one came down the middle. He got hold of it. McGraw just watched the ball sail out of the park.

"I think we've got a good piece of property," said Demaree.

"Yeah," said John J., but he didn't say anything to the Indian. McGraw was a hard man. He was one of the greatest managers baseball ever produced but he was a taskmaster. His men had to work. Work, work and more work, McGraw believed earnestly, made the great ballplayer. He had heard of the way Jim trained. He knew he would have to break him before he could build him into the kind of player he wanted. He knew, too, that it was going to be the toughest job he had ever handled.

In Marlin Springs Jim kept whacking the ball with no mean authority. Two days in a row Thorpe banged home runs against starting pitcher Wiltse. He was playing first base for the regulars, his screaming line drives winning the games against the scrub squad. In the first exhibition game of the season Jim got three hits in five trips to the plate. He batted fifth, got two singles, a double and also stole two bases. No one had seen anything like his speed on the bases. The Giants won that exhibition game—against Dallas, Texas—9-1.

"You're doing just fine," said George Burns, grabbing Thorpe's arm as they trotted into the clubhouse. "Keep it up, feller!"

John McGraw sang another tune.

"You'd better get down to the park in time!" he snapped.

"I wasn't late, was I?" asked Jim, innocently.

He had reported about five minutes before game time.

Tesreau smiled. Demaree smiled. Doyle laughed out loud.

McGraw turned on them, his face as red as a beet. The laugh stopped. Demaree and Tesreau turned away.

"You get down here with the rest of the club," shouted McGraw, "or you can go back to Carlisle!"

Anyone else on the club would have taken it, kept his mouth shut. But Jim didn't like the way McGraw said, "Carlisle."

He glared at the Little Napoleon.

"I can hit, can't I? I can throw, can't I? I can run, can't I? What do you want to do, see me sweat?"

"Yeah!" boomed John J. "I want to see you sweat!"

The story was the same in every town they hit, moving north back to New York. Jim was in the game, batting them out, covering his field, running them ragged on the base-paths, but he wasn't meeting with McGraw's idea of how a ballplayer should play the game.

"What time did you get in last night?" he demanded.

"In time to get to sleep," answered Jim.

"Too late!" spit John J. "Who was with you?"

"I left my little black book home," came back Thorpe.

McGraw glared but said nothing, turned on his heels and stormed into the rest of the squad.

"If any of you men want to spend your time closing the bars in the morning, get yourselves another club to play with! We're not going to win any pennants in a beer joint! We're going to win it playing ball!"

That was one of John J.'s biggest headaches. His club was rough and tough enough. They didn't need to be any tougher. But they took Jim Thorpe right into their camp—and keeping up with Jim was no cinch. The only difference was that Jim might do all right on his mad training schedule, but coming in at all hours, arriving at the park late and after an all-night binge wasn't going to do the rest of the club any good.

McGraw bore down harder on Jim; Jim became less and less responsive to the whiplash of the manager. It was only the three year contract at five thousand a year that stopped Mac from shipping the Indian straight out into some small farm team. He had to hold onto Thorpe as long as it was physically possible.

The Giants played Yale in its first April game of the season at the Polo Grounds. Jim was in the line-up. It wasn't because McGraw wanted him there. It was because he had to put him in. The Indian was the main attraction that afternoon and everyone knew it.

The men of Eli had a pretty good squad. They gave

# THE JIM THORPE STORY

the National-Leaguers quite a tussle. It was Jim Thorpe, in McGraw's doghouse, who spelled the difference between victory and defeat in that game.

The score was one to one when Jim came to bat. The boy pitching for Yale was doing a beautiful job. He pitched carefully to big Thorpe but not carefully enough. It was a high, fast one and Jim tagged it. It was the hardest-hit ball in the game, a ringing belt that hit the left field fence on a fly. The ball was hit so sharply that it caromed right back into the playing field. Only Jim's speed enabled him to make second on the blast. It was Jim's speed that made home plate on a beautiful slide with two men out. It was Jim's bat and his speed that won the game, 2 to 1.

The fans who had paid their good money to see the great Olympic star in a baseball uniform got their money's worth and more.

But that didn't bring any relief to the struggle between the manager and his ballplayer. Jim wasn't in the opening day line-up. He didn't get into a regular game until May 16th, and then only as a pinch hitter for pitcher Wiltse in the ninth inning of a game in which Hans Wagner hit a homer for the Pittsburgh Pirates.

Jim didn't like riding the baseball bench any more than he liked riding the football bench. But as long as he kept breaking training regulations McGraw wasn't going to use him as a regular. The struggle between the two men came to a sudden and dramatic end one afternoon early in the season, after the Giants had lost a close one and the boys were all on edge in the clubhouse.

"What are you paying me for?" demanded Jim of the already irritated McGraw.

"You've got a contract!"

"The contract is for playing ball!"

"You'll play ball for me when you're ready to toe the line, along with everybody else in the club!"

"I don't need your kind of beating to become a ball-player. I can play rings around anything you can show me. You're just a little wind trying to blow hard!"

McGraw was ready to burst wide open.

"Why you Indian. . . ."

Mac never finished.

Jim wouldn't take anybody calling him an Indian in any tone that even hinted the slightest disrespect.

"You. . . ."

He made a dash for the manager. Half the team intervened. Thorpe would have killed him if he had gotten his hands on him.

Demaree, Tesreau, Burns pulled Thorpe back, pinned down his arms. The rest of the club dragged the fiery McGraw into a back room and held him there.

"You shouldn't have done it, Jim," said Tesreau.

"Take it easy, Jim," said Burns.

"I'll bend him in two!" stormed Jim Thorpe. "I'll break him in half!"

But there was no further damage that afternoon, except that Jim was through with the Giants for the rest of the season. The next day he was shipped to New York's farm team in Milwaukee. There might have been a difference in Jim's career as a baseball player if he had landed with some other big-league team. John J. and Thorpe could never hit it off. They were too much alike—strong, stubborn, proud. One would never give ground to the other, and with McGraw the boss of the New York outfit it was Jim who had to go. If it weren't for the three-year contract the Indian would have been let go for good. But there was the contract . . . and the Irish in McGraw and the Indian in Thorpe would clash again, many times.

The Giants won the pennant that year, as was predicted, but it was another Indian, Chief Bender, pitching for the Athletics, who helped lick them in the World Series.

McGraw couldn't be blamed for his feelings about Thorpe. He certainly wasn't drawing the color line, which was still pretty strong those days, and it was at Mac's own invitation that Jim joined the Giants and White Sox on a world tour after the season was all over. Chief Meyers was in that troupe, along with Ivy Wingo, Christy Mathewson, Jeff Tesreau, Wiltse, Snodgrass, Leo Magee, Mike Dolan and Hans Lobert. Jim always loved to travel. He had good company on that world tour and he traveled as far as Japan, playing a game he loved to play. There was also the opportunity to forget some of the antagonism between the manager and the ballplayer. They never took advantage of it.

## fourteen

*T*HORPE WAS BACK WITH McGraw and the Giants at Marlin Springs, Texas in the spring of 1914. The old animosities were kept under control but they were still there, smoldering. Jim still ran those bases as fast as a deer and smacked the ball out to the fences with the same authority, but he never would consent to train the way McGraw wanted his men to train.

In a spring game with the San Antonio, Texas, club, Jim tried his hand at switch hitting. It was just another one of his pet tricks.

"What's he going to do next?" the Little Napoleon asked with quiet desperation.

But Jim got three hits that afternoon, two from the right side of the plate and the other from the port side.

In a game at Texarkana, a town right on the border of Texas and Arkansas, Jim slammed out three homers.

"I hit one home run inside the ball park," said the Indian. "That was one for Texas. I hit one over the right field wall and that landed in Arkansas. The third one," he added, "I belted over the left field wall into Oklahoma."

Jim smiled that big open smile of his.

"That made it three homers in one day for three different states."

Of course, the ball Jim hit over the left field fence would have had to catch a train to land in Oklahoma. Oklahoma is some forty miles from Texarkana. But Jim could hit them, and he knew it. If his records in the baseball books don't show it, they show why, too. The Indian just couldn't be disciplined by the hard-driving McGraw long enough to be kept in the line-up for any length of time. If the Little Napoleon couldn't discipline the easygoing Indian there was no one else in either league who could.

Jim Thorpe spent all but a few days of the 1914 season playing for Milwaukee. In 1915 he was sent by the New York club to Harrisburg, the former Newark franchise. McGraw had asked for waivers on the Indian but he couldn't get them. Jim was too great a potential star, besides being a tremendous drawing card. As soon as the word got about that the New York club was trying to get Thorpe out of the league the bids came pouring in. The Giants didn't at all like the idea of having the Indian play against them. McGraw shipped him off to the Pennsylvania farm club.

It was in Harrisburg that Jim struck up a quick friendship with the clown prince of baseball, Al Schacht. For a while they roomed together.

"Little Indian," Jim called Al Schacht.

"Big Indian," said Al Schacht.

Then they laughed, Jim slapping Al playfully on his back and almost knocking him out.

"We were playing Buffalo one afternoon," says Al Schacht. "Joe McCarthy, the great manager who piloted the Yankees to more than half a dozen championships, was playing second base for them. Joe Judge, who was to go up with the Senators, was playing first base. I was pitching against them, and in the early innings I was baffling the whole Buffalo team. They couldn't get more than ten or twelve runs off me.

"The first time Thorpe came up to the plate," continues the clown prince, "he got a great cheer from the crowd. Then I saw one of the funniest things I've ever seen on the diamond. Thorpe got hold of one and hit it through the box a mile a minute. Joe McCarthy raced over from second and stuck out his mitt for the ball. But that ball was really traveling. It hit the mitt, all right, smacked into it, knocked McCarthy back about three feet and pulled the glove away out into center field. There was McCarthy, picking himself up in a hurry, scrambing around for his glove, then scrambling for the ball which should have been somewhere in the infield but wasn't. When he finally collected himself, the Buffalo shortstop was holding the ball which had finally been whipped into the infield, the Buffalo right fielder was walking his glove back home, and Jim was

standing on third base, the grin on his face a mile wide.
McCarthy just looked at the Indian, then looked at his
glove. He was speechless."

This was the power behind the bat Jim Thorpe
waved at the plate. He got four for four that afternoon, two triples, a double and a single. The rumors
had it that the Indian could hit in the minors but not
in the majors, but when Jim got any time in the line-up
he could hit anywhere.

At Beaumont, Texas, April 1, 1916, the New York
newspapers sent out a release which was more of an
obituary than a sports story.

One paper reported:

An announcement made by Manager McGraw
tonight probably foreshadows the end of Jim Thorpe's
career as a major league ball player. After some tele-
graphic correspondence McGraw stated that he had
arranged to send the famous Indian athlete to the Milwaukee club of the American Association this season.
The New York club retains an option on Thorpe who
may be repurchased next fall if his record in the
American Association warrants further trial.

The Milwaukee club has asked for immediate de-
livery and Thorpe will probably sever his connection
with the Giant colts at Memphis next week.

Even Thorpe's best friends among the Giants hardly
hope that he will ever get out of the minors. He can
field and run bases, but he seems no further advanced

as a hitter than he was two years ago. He seems to hit fairly well in the minors, however, and he had an average of .298 with the Jersey City and Harrisburg teams of the International League last season.

To many friends, Thorpe has said that he intends to quit baseball if he cannot succeed as a big-leaguer. His services as a football coach are in great demand and he has a good-sized farm in Oklahoma which he paid for with money received from the New York club. Probably Thorpe would have been disposed of long ago but he held an unbreakable three-year contract and could not be cut off the pay roll. The New York club will pay perhaps two thirds of Thorpe's salary this season. He has been drawing $6,000 per year but this is the third and last season his contract is good. The Giants are all sorry to see the Olympic hero pass, as he was popular and never complained of his inability to hit big-league pitching.

The obituary, of course, proved too early. And Jim never "compained about his inability to hit big-league pitching" because he knew he could hit it, and he did, when given the chance. As for being cut adrift from the Giants, that prediction was still a few good years too soon.

In 1917 Jim played seven games on loan with the Cincinnati Reds, just long enough to play in and break up a game that has yet to be matched for sheer pitching brilliance in either of the major leagues.

It wasn't much of a crowd that came out to Chicago's

Weegman Park that afternoon. There was less than three thousand people in the stand. The Reds were playing host to the Chicago Cubs and no one was expecting anything spectacular. What they did see in that park that day was baseball history in the making. It started tamely enough but wound up in an atmosphere that even the seventh and deciding game of a World Series could scarcely approach for sheer tension and excitement.

Fred Toney was pitching for Cincinnati, the huge Jim Vaughn was in the box for Chicago. In the first inning both sides went down in order. In the second inning Fred Toney walked Cy Williams, who was playing center field for the Cubs, but the Bruins couldn't do anything else. The Reds went down in order again. The third, the fourth, the fifth, the sixth innings went by and the pitchers were pouring the ball over the plate beautifully. Not a man could whack that ball where no one could reach it. Not a man could belt out a hit. Heinie Groh, who was playing in a Red uniform that season, walked twice, but a couple of fast double plays eased Vaughn, the Cub pitcher, out of any possible trouble. Rollie Zeider fumbled a ball at short and Neale of Cincinnati reached first safely. He tried to steal second but this time the ball wasn't fumbled and he was out. In the fifth inning Fred Toney had walked Cy Williams again but no one else—no one on either team—could get anything else.

The crowd tensed as Toney toed the rubber for the

seventh inning. They sensed that they were witnessing an extraordinary performance. A no-hitter for two pitchers in one game was too much to expect. Some-one had to break. In the seventh inning it wasn't Fred Toney. The Cubs went down one, two, three. It wasn't Vaughn. The Reds went down one, two three. It was the same story in the eighth inning and again in the ninth. The crowd was glued to its seats. Never in the history of baseball had two pitchers pitched no-hit, no-run games for nine innings in one ball park. It was a feat that has yet to be repeated. Vaughn and Toney were magnificent.

Big Vaughn tossed in his warm-up pitches to start the tenth frame. The game was in overtime now. The catcher tossed the ball across the diamond to the second baseman. Vaughn was ready.

The first Redleg was Gus Getz. Vaughn retired him easily. There wasn't a sound in the stands. All Windy City was afraid to cheer, afraid to put the "whammy" on their pitcher.

Larry Kopf was the next batter. He looked at one, looked at another, then he swung his bat. The bat met the ball and the pellet sped like a rifleshot into right field. The crowd groaned, then it cheered wildly, but the cheer was not for Kopf who had gotten the first hit of the game, but for the great hurling of their pitcher.

However, that was all the cheering the Chicago fans were going to do for a while. Chase of the Redlegs was at bat. He let the first ball go, then whacked the next on a line to center. Williams of the Cubs had it, then dropped it. The strain was telling. Before the ball was back in the infield Kopf was on third.

The next batter was Jim Thorpe, on loan to Cincinnati, the man who, some said, could not hit big-league pitching.

"Get a piece of that ball, Jim," urged the Redleg manager, and Jim nodded, swinging his bat.

Vaughn pitched carefully. He knew there was power in that Indian bat, power enough to send out the long fly, the long belt which could send in Kopf from third.

A ball, a strike, another ball—then Jim swung. It wasn't a smash at the box. It wasn't a belt to the fences. It was a high, bouncing Baltimore chop, the kind of sock that hits the plate, or the territory near it, then bounces a mile up in the sky. Vaughn rushed to grab it. He turned toward first but he knew he could never catch the deer-footed Indian. He threw home. Too late, Kopf was across.

The Cubs came to bat in the last half of the tenth but they might as well have stayed at home. Fred Toney was invincible. He had pitched a ten-inning, perfect game. No runs and no hits. And the man who had won the game for him was the Sac and Fox Indian, the same one some Giant publicity man had written out of baseball much too soon.

Jim went back to the Giants in 1917, again in 1918 and 1919, but McGraw used him sparingly. The two big men never straightened out their feud; neither one would give the other an inch. The final blowup came early in the 1919 season. Jim was riding the bench again and a youngster by the name of Red Murray was patrolling the outfield. The game was a tight one. Murray was scheduled to hit but the Little Napoleon waved him back to the dugout and sent Jim in to pinch-hit.

The Indian had been storing up his anger for a long time. When Red Murray was put into the line-up Mc-Graw had more than hinted that he thought Jim wasn't good enough. Thorpe had taken more than enough from the little taskmaster. He was more than ready to pay back McGraw in kind.

"Why don't you let Murray hit?" he yelled back at the Little Napoleon, loud enough so that everybody in the park could hear him. "He can do much better for you than I can."

McGraw's face went red. It went redder as he watched Jim at the plate.

The first ball came a mile wide and Jim swung blindly. Swung is the wrong word. He just pushed his bat across the plate.

The second ball came across the plate and Jim swung again, but not at the ball.

There was a big grin on the Indian's face.

The third pitch he could have sent a mile out of the park, but that wasn't Jim's intention. He just waved his stick at it, as if he were saying good-by.

McGraw was the color of all the red roses in the world heaped into one basket. The bench was frozen, anticipating the fireworks, but Jim was all smiles.

"I told you," he said, blandly. "I told you Murray was a better man than Jim."

McGraw exploded.

"You've made a monkey of me, but you'll never do it again! You're through! Pack your bags and get out of here!"

Jim packed up, went to Boston, played in sixty games and ended the season with a .327 average in Beantown. This is not the kind of average a man who can't hit curve balls—which they said about Jim—can build up for himself in the major leagues.

In Boston Jim hit seven for seven as a pinch hitter, but Stallings, manager of the Braves, who had heard all about the Indian from McGraw, wasn't too eager to put him in the regular line-up. It was the long, loud and justified criticism from the Boston fans which finally forced his hand.

Stallings, of course, had his troubles. It was bad enough having one player who was tough to handle, but George Stallings had two. Rabbit Maranville was playing shortstop for the club and the Rabbit's zany antics are legion. Jim was a perfect partner for him. With the Giants, the Indian had put Tesreau out of action when he was sorely needed, just by playfully wrestling with him. Out in Harrisburg, Jim had held Al Schacht by his heels and playfully dangled him out of a twelfth-story window. These little tricks couldn't begin to compare with the mad jaunts the Rabbit and the Indian went on. If they weren't tossing water bags out of the hotel windows, like a couple of kids, they were jumping into pools, fully dressed, to catch goldfish. And the Rabbit could climb trees the way Jim had done as a boy in Oklahoma. Moonlight, of course, was the right light for climbing trees and for yowling like bobcats until the local police came dashing down to investigate the wild animal life.

While it was all good, clean fun for Jim, no manager could take it. It was Akron the next year, then Toledo and finally Portland, Oregon, where Jim hurt his arm sliding in a spring training game. There was one year of baseball left in the great athlete. He played for Hartford in the New England League for one year, then left the diamond for good.

Jim had a big-leaguer's heart. There weren't many who knew about it, however, because he played the game so easily. In 1917, when he was being bounced around by the New York club, Jim was undergoing an ordeal which would have broken almost anybody else's heart. But Jim played the game.

In 1913, shortly after he signed up the Giants, Thorpe married Iva Miller. It was a romance that had begun in Carlisle when Jim went back there at Warner's request. Iva was the daughter of a hotel man in Muskogee, Oklahoma, and she had attended the Chilocco Indian School before she transferred to Carlisle. At Chilocco her sister was a teacher.

"I'm Cherokee," said Iva, although Jim hadn't asked her.

Jim didn't talk much, nor did he ask many questions. The moment he met Iva he knew he wanted her for his wife. It took a mighty effort on his part to ask the question.

"I'm going off to play ball for New York," he began.

"I know," she said. She also knew there was something even more important on Jim's mind.

She took hold of Jim's big hand.

"Let's take a walk," she said.

They strolled silently out beyond the school grounds. They stopped under a giant oak tree.

"Jim," began Iva.

The night was clear, the sky was full of stars. In the distance they could see the small lights of Carlisle.

"There's something I have to tell you, Jim."

Jim didn't dare to look at her. He was afraid she was going to say "No" before he had even asked her.

"I'm not Indian," said Iva, abruptly. "I don't know why I never told you, but I'm not Indian, Jim. You'll forgive me, Jim?"

Jim looked at her for a long time before he spoke.

"Then I suppose you won't marry me," he said quietly.

"Marry you?" burst out Iva. "Marry you? Do you

want me to marry you, Jim?" She was beside herself with joy, but Jim didn't quite understand.

"You wouldn't marry an Indian, would you, Iva?"

It was Iva's turn to look into Jim's deep eyes. The tears began to course down her cheeks.

"I love you, Jim."

He put his big arms around her.

"I was afraid, Jim," she said, "afraid you wouldn't want to marry a girl who wasn't the Cherokee she said she was."

It was a happy marriage. They loved each other dearly, but Jim, the "loner," was hard for a woman to live with. There were three marriages in Thorpe's life, his first two wives remaining among his best friends and admirers even after divorce. But it was too much to ask of a woman to keep pace with the volatile life of the energetic Jim.

The first child born to them was a boy. He was named Jim, after his father, and looked like his father, too. Thorpe was crazy about the boy.

But in 1917 infantile paralysis struck and little Jim was killed by the dread disease.

Jim went wild. He disappeared. For days no one could find him. Then suddenly he was back in his playing uniform, outwardly the same grinning Jim Thorpe. No one knew the pain, the ache, the bewilderment the great star suffered. He got up for his turn at bat, he played the ball in the field, but his mind was miles away. First it had been his twin brother Charlie, then his mother, his father, and now his own son. His heart was almost broken but he played the game. Jim Thorpe was a great athlete, one of the greatest of all time. He was a man of great heart and courage, the kind of man who may lose a battle but never suffer defeat.

## fifteen

*J*IM THORPE WAS A much-better-than-average baseball player, good enough to play for the league champion Giants, for Cincinnati and the Boston Braves, but
it was the rougher, tougher, bruising sport of the gridiron which better suited the fighting spirit of the Sac
and Fox Indian. Even while he was being kicked around
by the New York Club, which never could quite make
up its mind about where to play the unpredictable Jim,
Thorpe never could forget the hundred yards which
stretched between the two sets of goal posts. All over
the country neither football players nor football fans
could ever forget the immortal Indian gridder.

In 1915 professional football was hot in the state
of Ohio. The Buckeye State had great pro teams in
Massillon, Cleveland, Akron, but there was always
room for one more. The Canton Bulldogs, orginally
organized away back in 1905, was being revived and
Jim Thorpe was offered five hundred dollars a game to
coach the team and play for it.

Jim didn't think twice about the offer. Nor was it

the money which pulled him back to the gridiron. He was just plain glad to get back into a football uniform, to get into a game in which some manager wasn't always after him, nagging him "foolishly" to stick to the training rules.

And those Canton Bulldogs were good. There was Peck, the All-American center from Pittsburgh; Jock Sutherland, the All-American guard, also from Pittsburgh, who was later to become one of America's greatest coaches; Fats Henry; Joe Guyon, the All-American halfback with both Carlisle and Georgia Tech; and Pete Calac, Little Twig and Long Time Sleep, all from the Indian school. It was a tough team, a fighting team, one of the really great professional squads of all time. In 1922 they won ten, tied two and lost none. In 1923 they won eleven, tied one and lost none. Those Canton Bulldogs established a pro record which has never been equaled.

It was in a game between the Bulldogs and the Massillon Tigers, another of Ohio's immortal professional clubs, that Jim Thorpe met the great Kenneth Knute Rockne, the immigrant lad from Denmark who was to coach Notre Dame to football history.

The Rock was a newcomer to the professional game. He was All-American end at Notre Dame and captained the team, but he knew that he had never played against anyone like the already legendary Jim Thorpe. He looked at the Indian as he threw the ball around and kicked a few before the whistle for the opening kickoff. There was six feet two inches of him, all solid, and Knute knew, too, that the Indian liked to run around the ends.

The Rock gritted his teeth.

"Big guy or no," he said to himself, "nobody is going to cut around my end in this game."

Knute always had what it takes to make a good football man—vigor, stamina, courage. He wasn't a big fellow, as gridders go, but he made up for his size with determination and aggression. He didn't know what fear was, and in the very first plays of the game he hurled himself at the big man, stopped him cold. Rockne wasn't stepping aside for any man.

Jim picked himself up from the gridiron, looked admonishingly at the mighty mite.

"You shouldn't do that to Old Jim," he said to the unsmiling Rock. "All of those people sitting in the stands paid just to see Old Jim run."

"Go ahead and run," came back the stony-faced Rockne. "Go ahead and run, if you can."

The Rock was pretty cocky. He was doing better than holding his own with the great legend of the gridiron.

Two, three, four more times in that first quarter Thorpe tried to skirt Rockne's end, but Knute was there all the time and the Indian wasn't gaining enough to measure—if he wasn't actually being shoved back.

Jim was always a patient fellow but there was a limit to his kindness.

When the second quarter was only minutes old, Jim issued his final warning.

"All those people paid to see Jim run," he said. "You've got to let Old Jim run."

The Rock had his own ideas about what the people had paid for and he was beginning to feel pretty smug about the way he had Thorpe stopped. This time he allowed himself a little smile as he repeated his first invitation.

"Go ahead and run, if you can."

It was a little smile the Rock allowed himself. It was his last smile that afternoon.

On the very next play Jim came tearing around end again. The Rock dived for him, hard, hard enough to stop even the best of them. But Old Jim was going to run this time. He had given the young fellow plenty of time to consider the customers. With the pigskin safely tucked under his arms, the Indian gave him the old hip and knee and the Rock went sprawling into the Massillon bench, ending up among the water buckets. Old Jim? He was off and down the field, sixty yards for a touchdown.

The grin was big on his face as he trotted back down to the Massillon bench. He looked at the Rock, still too dazed to know what had hit him.

"That was nice work," said Jim. "You let Old Jim run."

It was while Thorpe was playing with the Canton Bulldogs that he also met Ernie Nevers, the great Stanford fullback who was later to coach the Chicago Cardinals. Pop Warner, who coached both Nevers and Thorpe, never could make up his mind about who was the greater of the two. He once picked Ernie Nevers but felt he had to make some sort of explanation for it.

"I could always get sixty minutes of football out of Nevers," he said, "but I could never get more than twenty minutes a game out of the Indian."

Recalling what that Indian did in twenty minutes against such great teams as Harvard, Pennsylvania and Army, sixty minutes of football with Thorpe should have been something no human being could take on the gridiron.

Gil Dobie, who coached championship teams at Cornell, the University of Minnesota and the University of Washington, where he established a record of fifty-eight wins and two ties against no defeats, was drilling the North Dakota Aggies when he first saw Jim Thorpe in action. Years later he was watching the brilliant Doc Blanchard of Army moving that pigskin down the field, and someone asked him how he would rate the cadet.

Dobie didn't have to think to answer.

"The only man who could make him play second string," he said, "would be Jim Thorpe."

The argument about Jim and Ernie Nevers has rocked back and forth over many years. It is one of those debates that can't be settled. It's like asking who was the greatest heavyweight champion of the world,

Jack Dempsey, Joe Louis or Jack Johnson. Thorpe, who played against Nevers, says, "All I know is that I would hate to try to beat Ernie out for fullback when he was in his prime, and I still have to meet the man who, in my opinion, could have kept me on the bench as halfback."

Ernie Nevers, on his part, has nothing but the greatest respect for Jim Thorpe's prowess, a respect bordering on awe. He will never forget the first time he played against the great Sac and Fox Indian. Jim was nearly forty at the time, in the twilight of his magnificent career, and Nevers just out of school, young and fresh.

It was toward the end of the game. Jim was going down the field for a long pass. Ernie Nevers was covering him all the way. It was a cold day, the ground icy but firm. The two men moved at a quick, tense clip. Suddenly, Ernie Nevers went up in the air for the pigskin and Jim came charging in.

"He hit me solidly," says Nevers. "He hit me solidly in the chest with his shoulder and I went skidding. I felt as though all my ribs had caved in, and I lay stunned on the ground."

Normally, Ernie would have remained there where he finally stopped skidding.

"I'd have taken my two minutes of rest," he says, "because I certainly needed them."

But with Jim Thorpe playing against you, there is no rest. Before he could move, Jim Thorpe reached down and grasped the stunned Nevers by the hand, pulled him up to his feet.

"Are you all right, young fellow?" he asked.

Ernie wasn't all right. There were bells still ringing in his head and his chest felt like it would never come back to normal. But Ernie is a pretty tough man—and with Jim grinning into his face, all he could do was to try to manage a grin which just wouldn't come.

"Sure, Jim," said Nevers, trying to get a deep breath down into his lungs. "I'm O.K.," he said, and to himself, "Brother! I'm glad I wasn't playing against this Indian ten years ago!"

And Jim smiled.

"How can anybody get hurt playing football?" he always asked and, strange as it may have seemed to all the guards, tackles, ends, centers and backs who had ever had the good or bad fortune to meet up with him when he was carrying the ball or trying to stop someone else who was carrying the ball, the Indian really meant it.

Steve Owen, the big, affable coach of the New York (football) Giants, has his own story on the terrific power Jim Thorpe could generate on the professional football field.

Steve was fresh out of college and playing his first game as a pro. As fortune would have it, the Indian was playing with the opposition and Steve, playing tackle, was going to meet up with dynamic Thorpe in a series of damaging encounters. However, contrary to Steve's expectations the afternoon started calmly enough.

Steve Owen, weighing a good two hundred and forty pounds, charged into the line on the very first play, and Jim, instead of blocking, nodded in Owen's direction. Steve didn't stop to consider the invitation. He just plunged at the fellow carrying the ball and threw him for a loss.

"I felt prety cocky about that," says Steve Owen, recalling the day, "and I thought that maybe Jim had gotten old and wasn't too eager about blocking any more".

On the next play Steve grew bolder, maybe a little brasher. He didn't wait for Jim's signal this time. He just brushed the Indian away and brought the runner down again, for another loss.

Steve was completely sure of himself by now. He felt that the Indian was just about finished. He didn't have to worry about him any more. Jim Thorpe may have been a great blocking back once. He certainly wasn't going to do much blocking with Steve Owen doing the tackling. That's what Steve Owen thought. And that's the way he acted, preparing himself for the next play.

"I got ready for a real tackle," he says. "I shifted wider for a better shot, never bothering with the Indian."

That was a mistake.

Steve plunged for the ball carrier and—how or why

he didn't know—there he was, landing squarely on top of his head.

"I didn't know where I was or what had happened until Old Jim dragged me to my feet," says the smiling Steve Owen.

"Young man," warned Jim, beginning to give the astonished Owen a very quick and very short football lesson, "never take your eyes off the wing back."

When he wanted to play, Jim was the best man who ever donned a football uniform. When he wanted to run, he ran. When he wanted to block, he was little less than brutal. When he wanted to tackle, he was little short of murder.

The Canton Bulldogs were a great team with Thorpe, but Jim calls the Oorang Indians, a team he assembled, the best of the lot and one of the greatest professional teams that ever played on the gridiron.

Four Carlisle captains played with the Oorang Indians. Jim Thorpe, Busch, Calac and Guyon were in its line-up, with Thorpe, Guyon and Calac in the backfield. Red Fox of the Haskel Institute was quarterback, Long Time Sleep and Bill Newaska its tackles, Busch and Hill its guards, Nason and Chief Little Twig its ends. This was a team to strike terror in any squad that opposed it. Jim Thorpe, of course, was the spark in any aggregation of gridders. He was the man who could spell the difference between victory and defeat. And if Jim was in the mood there could be only one result: victory.

## sixteen

*O*N A HOT SEPTEMBER AFTERNOON in Canton, Ohio, on September 17, 1920, a handful of young men with considerable vision, as far as sports are concerned, met together in the showroom of an automobile agency run by Ralph Hays. Hays was then manager of the Canton Bulldogs. The purpose of the meeting was to discuss the possibilities of a football association patterned after the big leagues in baseball.

The men sat around on the fenders of the shiny new cars and talked football for a long time. They knew what they were talking about, too. There was a lot of interest in the professional game throughout the country. There was a demand for organized league competition. When the boys got through talking, the American Professional Football Association was born. The vice-president of the new organization was Stan Cofall, the brilliant Notre Dame captain, then playing ball for the Massillon Tigers. The president of the organization was the great Jim Thorpe.

Listed in the American Professional Football Association were the Staleys; the Canton Bulldogs; the Cleveland Indians; the Dayton Triangles; the Akron Professionals; the Massillon Tigers; Rochester, New York; Rock Island, Illinois; Muncie, Indiana; the Chicago Cardinals; and Hammond, Indiana.

Professional football had been played for a long time before this first effort to organize professional football leagues; and, curiously, it was Connie Mack of the baseball Philadelphia Athletics who claimed the first professional football championship of the United States. His team, also called the Philadelphia Athletics, with the Hall of Fame pitcher Rube Waddell in a gridder's togs, defeated Pittsburgh—with the lengendary Christy Mathewson playing in the backfield. This, Connie decided, was enough to establish his championship claim. There were others who claimed rights to the football crown with even less evidence of prowess on the gridiron. The laurels of the champion, however, could be decided only through organized competition between the best teams that could be assembled in all parts of the country. The establishment of the American Professional Football Association was the logical step to be taken by the professional gridders. It wasn't a perfect setup but it gave the game a terrific impetus. It was only logical that the first president of the association should be the greatest of all football players, the Indian Jim Thorpe.

Jim played up and down the association and later

moved among the less powerful leagues and teams. He started with the Canton Bulldogs, organized the Oorang Indians in La Rue, Ohio, played with the Rock Island Independents in 1922, 1923 and 1924. In 1925 Jim played with the New York Giants again. This time it wasn't baseball, it was football, but he was going to run into some of that old Giant trouble again.

Thorpe was thirty-seven years old at the time. Thirty-seven years isn't just old on the gridiron, it's ancient. As a matter of fact, when a man is thirty-seven he rarely dares compete in any athletic contest. Some of the marathon runners have actually won the event when they've been that old, but marathon running doesn't demand the brutal bodily contact of other sports, like boxing, hockey, baseball and especially football. A pitcher in the big leagues can hang around, hurling every once in a while, until he is forty, but very few do. Sammy Baugh still pitches his forward passes on the gridiron but he isn't in there to block, to tackle, to run with the ball, and his appearances in the game are less and less frequent and for shorter and shorter intervals. Yet Sammy isn't as old as Jim Thorpe was when the Indian was banging into the line, smashing into his opposition, stretching them out cold for the New York (football) Giants.

In the opening game of the season the Giants rolled up a 26-0 victory over New Britain. In the first quarter they struck twice for the touchdown; the first was made by Jack McBride who just the year before had been the leading point maker in the country, scoring one hundred points for Syracuse. The other touchdown was made from scrimmage by that young oldster, the irrepressible Jim Thorpe.

But, just a little more than three weeks later, Jim got his walking papers. The Giants were releasing him. The reason: failure to get into proper playing condition.

John McGraw had said the same thing, in different words. Jim was just a bit careless about training.

The release from the New York club sent Jim back to Rock Island. It looked like curtains for the thirty-seven-year-old Indian, but the curtains were slow in descending on the performance of America's greatest athlete. In January of the following year Jim was playing football with the professional club of St. Petersburg, Florida. Jim was now thirty-eight, or just a few months short of it.

St. Petersburg was playing Winter Haven. It wasn't going to be a great game and normally the clubs would not expect a huge crowd to fill the park. But Jim, who was used to seeing thousands of people fill the stands just to see him run, looked at the stands, almost counted the less than three hundred fans who had come out for the game, and turned sadly away.

Although Jim was an old man as far as the game was concerned, with the pigskin in his hands he was sure to turn in a brilliant moment, a magnificent run, a damaging block, a brilliant kick. He never failed to show the

THE JIM THORPE STORY

fans a glimpse of the Thorpe who was the terror of the gridiron, to remind them that they were looking at a man who had made sport history.

At St. Petersburg he punted twice for sixty-five yards, punts men in their prime could not equal. And he tried a drop kick once from the fifty-yard stripe. It missed. It missed by inches and the three hundred fans stood up in the stands to cheer. But they were not cheering for the team from Winter Haven. They were not cheering a drop kick that failed. They were cheering for the man, Jim Thorpe, who had written his name big in the story of American athletics.

It was a sad man who waved farewell to the cheering stands as he walked back into the dressing room after the final whistle of the game.

"I guess I'm finished," he said to the reporters who came back to talk with him. "I always played because I love the game. I like to play, to compete. I guess I'll go back to my people now—to hunt and fish with them."

But Jim wasn't through yet, not by a few years.

In 1927 he was playing with his old Canton Bulldogs again. He was with Portsmouth, Ohio, in 1928, with Hammond, Indiana, in 1929. In that same year Jim played for the Chicago Cardinals. He was forty-one. While he still had plenty of power in his arms and legs, no man of forty-one can take the punishment of the gridiron. Jim played his last game of football that year in a game between the Cardinals and the Bears.

No one likes to see the champion slow down, no one likes to see some youngster who wasn't good enough to lace his shoes push him around. There were many wet eyes among the fans in that last game—and the wettest were those of his old friends who remembered so well the great days of Carlisle, the early days of the Canton Bulldogs, the Indian, who with his own skill and courage, had fashioned a niche for himself in the heart of every American who loves the aggressive, the tough, the hard, the never-say-die athlete.

*O*RGANIZED BASEBALL and organized football were both a matter of record and history for the once-invincible Thorpe now. A man past forty cannot hope to crash the line-ups of the young and powerful professional teams competing on the diamond or the grid-iron. Jim took a long time realizing the facts, however, the physical facts. He took a longer time accepting them. He could drop an Ernie Nevers like a ton of bricks when Nevers was in his twenties and Jim in his late thirties. He could still kick a ball more than half the length of the field when he was past forty. Even at sixty, the huge crowds that came to see the Forty-niners of San Francisco play in Kezar Stadium watched the wonderful Thorpe boot them over the goal from the mid-field stripe. There was plenty of power left in the Indian when he departed from professional ball, but he knew at long last that his greater days of glory were something for the memory now, something to talk about, something to recall with deserving pride, but nothing more.

Still, Jim could not tear himself away from the world of sports. In 1930 he joined C. C. Pyle and his cross-country marathon. Jim didn't run. He was Pyle's master of ceremonies. The marathon derby was well nicknamed the bunion derby and C. C. Pyle was rightfully called Cash and Carry. Pyle and the marathon venture went broke, and the once-mighty Jim Thorpe had to sue Mr. Pyle for the fifty dollars that was coming to him. Jim had earned a tremendous amount of money in both baseball and football. With McGraw he had received the then fabulous salary of five thousand dollars a year for three seasons running. In professional football he had started with a contract calling for five hundred dollars a game with the Canton Bulldogs, and then built up his income on the gridiron till he was getting an average of fifteen thousand dollars a year from the game.

But Jim had always been easy with his money. Besides, by 1930 he had quite a little family to support. In 1926 the Sac and Fox had married for the second time. His wife was Frieda Kirkpatrick, a Scotch-Irish girl, the daughter of a golf club manager. They had four children, all boys—Phil, Bill, Dick and Jack. Phil, who is twenty-three now, is with the Army Intelligence Service. Bill, who is twenty-two, works in a steel plant on the West Coast. Dick, seventeen, and Jack, thirteen, are at school in Oregon.

"Phil can run the hundred-yard dash in ten seconds," says Jim with some pride. "He played football for his Army team," he adds. "Quarterback. A little like Old Jim."

Dick is a runner.

"He wants to become a decathlon man," says the old warrior, and a distant smile comes to his mouth. "He wants to win back my trophies."

In 1930, however, the depression had hit our country pretty hard. There were millions of people who couldn't find any work. Men who had held down good jobs were selling apples in the street to earn what few pennies they could. There were bread lines for the hungry and some people were forced to build themselves flimsy lean-tos on vacant lots because there was nothing they could do about paying rent. There wasn't much call for the kind of work Jim Thorpe could do.

For a while in 1930 he tried painting, the kind of painting he had learned at the Carlisle school. In 1931 the Universal Studios in Hollywood hired him to play Chief Black Crow in a routine movie. He also did some work on a baseball picture for Merto-Goldwyn-Mayer. There was also a short on football in which he worked with his great coach Glenn Warner. But the movies, too, were taking it on the chin from Old Man Depression and even as early as March 4, 1931, the newspapers had an item about Jim Thorpe working as a day laborer at four dollars a day, using a pick and shovel, helping to lay the foundation for the new Los Angeles County Hospital.

There is nothing wrong with using a pick and shovel to make your living, but the four dollars a day was a long cry from the five hundred a game and the fifteen thousand a season which Thorpe had earned only a few years back. Only the indomitable will of the Sac and Fox—his magnificent aggressive spirit—could have kept the fighting Indian going in these tough circumstances. Philip was four and Billy just two at the time. Children have to eat and they were going to eat—as long as Papa Thorpe could wield that old pick and shovel.

Still, in spite of all the adversity, Jim dreamed on. At a press interview he spoke of the possible return of the old Carlisle star to the gridiron wars.

"I guess it's an old story," he said to the newspaper reporter. "I liked to be a good fellow with the boys. But I'll come out of this, you can be sure."

There was talk of his going to Dickinson College at Carlisle to act as all-round coach. There was talk of his dickering for a post at Mississippi A. and M.

"I think I'd rather be back at Carlisle. I don't have to tell you why. I've got a lot of memories back in Carlisle. In the meantime, the pick and shovel will have to do."

No, Jim was down but he was a long way from being

beaten. He even began to talk about getting back those trophies he had won at the Stockholm Olympics.

"Ballyhoo," answered one A.A.U. official.

"He's just looking for publicity," said another.

But the people, the fans, held another opinion, one which they demonstrated wildly at the 1932 Olympic Games which took place in Los Angeles.

Jim almost missed those games. He didn't have a ticket. That is the way with the world of sports. One day a man is a hero, the next day he is a goat. One day he is king of all athletes, the next day he is forgotten.

Somehow or other, however, the story broke. Jim Thorpe can't get in to see the Olympics. He hasn't got a ticket.

The reaction was immediate and overwhelming. From all parts of the country protests flowed into the offices of the A.A.U. and into the newspaper offices. Thousands of people, just the everyday, ordinary fans, offered their own tickets to the man who had been the hero of the 1912 American squad at Stockholm. It was a magnificent demonstration of the loyalty of America's Joe Doak to his greatest athlete. Jim Thorpe wasn't leaving them behind on the track any more. He wasn't spilling them all over the gridiron. But he was still there, where the American fan keeps his memories, his admiration and his love for the great competitor.

No one, however, had to give up his precious seat

at the Los Angeles Olympics. Any man would have been proud to say, "Jim Thorpe sat in my seat at the Olympic Games." One man said, "Jim sits with me."

That man was Vice-president of the United States, Charles Curtis. There was Indian blood, too, in the veins of the man who was second only to the President of our country. No Indian who had brought such honors to our land would be slighted, not as long as Charles Curtis held office.

Jim Thorpe sat in the presidential box at the 1932 Olympics, and the more than one hundred thousand fans who crowded the stadium rose in one mighty ovation to the athlete whose record is without equal in the history of American sport.

But this, like a flash flood, was there and gone with the moment. Every once in a while someone is reminded of Thorpe and then there is another story, perhaps a dinner at which Jim sits and hears stories about his past glories and is politely, even enthusiastically, applauded for them. The moment arrives, goes as quickly, and then Jim gets down to work again, the work of making a living for himself and for his family.

In 1933 he brought suit against the Columbia Picture Corporation for using his name and picture to advertise the film, "The White Eagle" in which he did not appear.

In 1933, too, there was a news item from Hollywood about Jim's being thrown from a horse in the shooting of a picture at the Warner-First National studios, where he was hired as an extra for a picture called "Telegraph Trail."

Jim Thorpe could break in a bucking colt when he was not quite fifteen years old. But now time was slipping away from the magnificent athlete. Except for an occasional note in the papers, he was being forgotten.

He worked as a supervisor of recreation in the Chicago parks. He worked as a guard for the Henry Ford River Rouge automobile plant. He toured the country to give lectures on football. He wore his feather headdress and talked to audiences of his own magnificent career. Wherever he went he always commanded the respect and admiration of his listeners, but lecturing was never easy for the fighting Indian. He had always preferred the battlefield of physical conflict to the debate with words. During World War II he tried to enlist for active service but he was turned down because of his age. In 1941, after Pearl Harbor, Jim was fifty-three. He wasn't too old, however, to be taken by the Merchant Marine and to sail that most dangerous of cargoes, live munition, clear around to far-off India.

In 1945, in the last year of the war, Jim married again, for the third time. He met Patricia Askew when he was wearing the football uniform of the Rock Island Independents. Even at that time Patricia was one of Jim's most ardent admirers. A chance meeting, almost thirty years later, in Lomita, California, proved the beginning of a new and lasting relationship for them. Patricia, now Mrs. Jim Thorpe, is not only an ardent admirer of her husband's, she is one of the most earnest and persistent campaigners for the return of those Stockholm Olympic trophies to their rightful owner.

There always has been talk about getting those prizes back to the United States. Occasionally there is an article in the papers, or in some magazine, and once in a while someone makes a real mission of it.

Back in March, 1943, a resolution was introduced into the Oklahoma House of Representatives, calling for A.A.U. to return "Big Jim's" medals and demanding that all his records be restored to the official books.

D. M. Madrano, president of the Caddo Tribal Council and a representative from Tulsa, went further. He asked the state to do something for its famous son and urged that Thorpe be appointed to direct athletics in one of Oklahoma's colleges.

Bill Corum, Dan Parker, James A. Burchard and a host of sports writers and columnists have run reams of paper on the subject from time to time. Leon (Chief) Miller, lacrosse coach at the College of the City of New York (C.C.N.Y.), carried a vigorous campaign all on his own over a long period of time, blasting away at the A.A.U. and its purer-than-pure rulings. Miller is a Cherokee Indian and was a classmate of Thorpe's at Carlisle.

Blasted Chief Miller:

In the light of modern practices in so-called amateur sports, Jim Thorpe was the victim of a terrible injustice

that should be righted while there is still time. Income
tax reports of some of our leading amateur athletes
would emphasize the point I am trying to make. Jim
Thorpe was such a thorough amateur in every sense of
the word that when the small-town Pennsylvania
sports writer dug up the fact that Jim had received $15
for playing a few Sunday ball games during the summer vacation, he confirmed the fact, immediately.
Thorpe spoke the truth, just as any man with a clear
conscience would. And because he received $15 or
thereabouts and wouldn't lie about it, his athletic
career was ruined.

Jim's athletic career wasn't completely ruined, of
course, but Chief Miller's anger is easy to understand.
There is scarcely a fan today who doesn't believe
wholeheartedly that all of Jim's records belong in the
official books. There is hardly a fan who doesn't want
that Viking ship and the sculptured head of the King
of all Sweden sitting in Jim's parlor.

But Jim, Jim just keeps moving along.

"Sure I'd like all those trophies," he says, a twinkle
in his eyes. "But I guess I'm just too busy working at
making a living to bother much about them."

When the Israeli National Soccer Team arrived in
this country on its tour of friendship, Jim Thorpe was
selected to train the squad which had come to us from
the new nation.

He managed and toured with his own girls' team,
the Thunderbirds, in the National Softball Congress.

"A good team," says Jim, with real manager's pride.

Occasionally you will find him on a golf course, doing the eighteen holes under a hundred with just a single club and a putter.

The old athlete goes on.

In 1950, before he had reached his sixty-second birthday, there was suddenly a new rush of clipping on Thorpe. Pictures of the warrior appeared in every newspaper, in thousands of magazines. There were new stories about his life, about the great name he had made for himself and his country in every sport Americans play at and compete in. As if he had not won enough medals and trophies in his years on the diamond, on the track, on the gridiron, a series of new trophies were awarded to him. A movie of his life was being rushed into production. Jim Thorpe, in January and February of 1950 again began to make Page One in the sports world.

Perhaps Jim Thorpe was really going to get back his Olympic medals. Or was this sudden outpouring of eulogies an even greater reward?

## eighteen

ITH New Year's Day, 1950, the twentieth
century had reached the halfway mark and sport writers all over the country began to take count of just what
had been accomplished in those fifty years. Who had
been the country's greatest runners? Who had been
its greatest baseball players? Who had been the bright
stars on the gridiron.

On January 25, 1950, the New York *Times* ran a
banner headline:

## THORPE HAILED AS GREATEST PLAYER
## ON GRIDIRON IN PAST FIFTY YEARS

It was a headline splashed across every sport sheet
in the country—and once again Jim Thorpe was the
brilliant halfback, the magnificent runner, blocker, kicker, the single greatest threat on the football field. The
subhead read:

## CARLISLE INDIAN FIRST IN MID-CENTURY POLL WITH 170 VOTES

Youngsters who knew Thorpe only from what they had heard about him began to pour over the columns and columns of newsprint on the brilliant athlete. Old-timers let their chest spread with pride and wiped away a tear, remembering the old days when Jim could bull his way through any squad the great Harvard, Pennsylvania, Pittsburgh or Army could mass against him.

"Thorpe combined the Irishman's love of combat, which he inherited from his father, with the Indian's cunning and grace," they read, "to gain his place in the sport's hall of fame in 1911 and 1912, playing left halfback for the now-defunct Carlisle, Pennsylvania, Indian School."

Carlisle was only a memory now, but Jim was as big as life again wherever people talked about the game.

"None of the modern players, wrote the sports writers, "benefited by the game's amazing growth through the intervening four decades, could nudge the six-foot-two-inch Sac and Fox warrior from first place."

The Associated Press had taken a poll among sports writers and broadcasters all over the country. One hundred and seventy of them had voted Jim the greatest football star of the twenty century. The nearest man to him was Harold (Red) Grange, the Galloping Ghost of Illinois, with an amazing record which includes the gaining of five hundred and twenty-four yards with tweny-seven passes; touchdown runs of seventy yards against Nebraska, ninety-two yards against Northwestern, sixty yards against Chicago, four touchdown runs of ninety yards, sixty-five yards, forty-five yards and fifty-five yards, all in the first ten minutes of play against Michigan, ninety-four yards against Iowa and ninety-four yards against Chicago. Yet Red Grange, the terror of the Chicago Bears, trailed Jim Thorpe with one hundred and thirty-eight votes, thirty-two less than the mighty Indian.

From there, the votes amassed by the gridiron greats dropped sharply. Bronko Nagurski, Minnesota's All-American Iron Man, the only man to win places on All-American teams in two positions, at tackle and at halfback, who rose to even greater heights in professional ball as a tremendous line crasher and blocking back, received a scant thirty-eight votes.

In fourth spot on the poll, with just seven votes, was the Stanford giant, Ernie Nevers, the man who is often compared in football circles to the towering Indian, Jim Thorpe.

Tied with Ernie Nevers with seven votes was Slinging Sammy Baugh of Texas Christian University and the professional Washington Redskins. Baugh, one of the most magnificent passers in the history of football, is still active at the ripe gridiron age of thirty-six.

In the sixth slot of the Associated Press poll was Don Hutson of the University of Alabama and later the Green Bay Packers, one of the most brilliant pass receivers in the sport. Don received just six votes.

The immortal George Gipp of Notre Dame, one of the game's most sensational broken field runners, got four votes.

Charlie Trippi, the Georgia Flash, still playing great ball in the professional ranks, received three votes.

Receiving two votes in the poll were Columbia University's Sid Luckman, who wrote his name big in the history of the Chicago Bears; Steve Van Buren of Louisiana State; Willie Heston of the University of Michigan; and Ohio State's famous Chick Harley.

With one vote each came Bill Henry of Washington and Jefferson College; Bennie Oosterbaan, Michigan's brilliant All-American end, now coaching the Wolverines; Iowa's glamorous Niles Kinnick, killed in action in the last war; the triple threat, Glenn Dobbs of Tulsa; Glenn Davis, the Mr. Outside of Army's undefeated elevens; Clyde (Bulldog) Turner of Hardin Simmons and professional ball; Doak Walker of Southern Methodist; Frankie Albert, the magician of the T-formation at Stanford; Doc Blanchard, the Mr. Inside of the great cadet teams; and the sensational dropkicker, the immortal Charlie Brickley of Harvard.

But leading the list, head and shoulders above everybody else in the field, stood Jim Thorpe. His was a title well earned and well deserved. The country sat up and took notice again of the man who had brought his native land athletic glory that has never been equaled in its history.

Jim was feted everywhere. Athletes and fans throughout the country gathered to pay homage to him. Once again Jim Thorpe was the Number One athlete in his country.

Once again Hollywood awoke to the tremendous popularity of the Indian star. But this time the Sac and Fox wasn't going to be used as an extra in some class D wild west serial. This time it would be Jim Thorpe, the country's greatest athlete, the hero of the American people.

Twenty-five thousand dollars went to the Indian for the rights to screen the movie of his life. The Warner Brothers' movie lots began to get ready for production. Burt Lancaster was signed to play the role of Thorpe, Charles Bickford the role of Pop Warner. Other actors signed up for the picture were Steve Cochran and Phyllis Thaxter, who plays Mrs. Thorpe. Top sports writer from the Coast, Vincent Flaherty, and Douglas Morrow were assigned to write the script for the movie, and Michael Curtiz to direct.

Jack Warner, of Warner Brothers, announced that the picture would cost one million dollars to produce. Warner has always loved to do stories that were strictly American in feeling, stories of the building of the West, stories of the people who make the headlines.

"Jim Thorpe is all American," Jack Warner declared for the press. "His story is all American. It is the kind of story which could have happened only here, in our country."

But there were still more honors due the magnificent athlete. For once a country was honoring its hero while he still was alive. On February 12, 1950, the newspapers ran a second banner headline about the big athlete:

THORPE NAMED GREATEST IN SPORT

The Associated Press again had polled sports writers and broadcasters throughout the nation. Three hundred and ninety-three ballots went out to every important commentator on athletics, from Miami, Florida, to Bar Harbor, Maine, from Los Angeles on the Pacific Coast to New York on the Hudson. Two hundred and fifty-two named Jim Thorpe the greatest athlete of the first fifty years of the twentieth century. Babe Ruth, whose contribution to big-time baseball may never be equaled, drew eighty-six first places. Jack Dempsey, whose fists built the million-dollar fight gates, pulled nineteen first places. Ty Cobb received eleven; the Brown Bomber, Joe Louis, five; the lovable Lou Gehrig, four; the Galloping Ghost, Red Grange, three; Jackie Robinson, who broke the color line in baseball, two; Bobby Jones, golf immortal, two; Bronko Nagurski and Big Train, Walter Johnson, and Cornelius Warmerdam, brilliant pole vaulter, one each. There was no question in the minds of the sports people as to who stood like a giant above everyone else in the world of athletics. Two out of every three who voted named Jim Thorpe the greatest of them all. When all the points were counted in the one-two-three poll, Jim had amassed eight hundred and seventy-five points. It was like the old track and field days when the Indian used to run up the great scores for little Carlisle. It was like the old days on the gridiron when Jim used to gain more ground in the rushes than the entire team on the opposition. It resembled the old days at Stockholm where Jim carted home the trophies for the low score of seven in the pentathlon, the unbelievably high score of well over eight thousand in the decathlon.

The closest approach to Jim's eight hundred and seventy-five points was made by Babe Ruth with five hundred and thirty-nine. From there the drop was fast. Dempsey pulled two hundred and forty-six; Ty Cobb one hundred and forty-eight; Bobby Jones eighty-eight; Joe Louis seventy-three; Red Grange fifty-seven; Jesse Owens, the great sprinter of the Berlin Olympics, fifty-four; Columbia's Lou Gehrig thirty-four; Nagurski twenty-six; Jackie Robinson twenty-four; Bob Mathias, the eighteen-year-old winner of the decathlon at the London Olympics, thirteen; Walter Johnson twelve; Glenn Davis, of Army fame, eleven; William Tilden, the tennis great, nine; the magnificent track man, Glenn Cunningham, eight; Glen Morris eight; and Cornelius Warmerdam seven.

Jim's total was almost as great as the combined score of the next three men in the poll. Except for Babe Ruth's, his total points almost equaled the combined points of every other man named by the sports writers and broadcasters. Jim Thorpe's magnificence as a sport figure is almost unbelievable.

There has never been an athlete on the American scene, on the world scene, to equal the versatility, the prowess, the vigor, the fighting spirit, the sheer ability of Jim Thorpe. There will be athletes who will be compared to Bright Path, and the comparison will do them honor. There never will be another Jim Thorpe.

## JIM THORPE'S TRACK AND FIELD RECORDS

| | |
|---|---|
| 100-yard dash (Carlisle) | 10 seconds |
| 100-yard dash (practice sprint at Carlisle) | 9.8 seconds |
| 120-yard high hurdles | 15 seconds |
| 220-yard low hurdles | 23.8 seconds |
| 440-yard race | 51 seconds |
| 1,500 meter run | 4 minutes 40.1 seconds |
| High jump | 6 ft. 5 in. |
| Broad jump | 23 ft. 6 in. |
| Pole vault | 10 ft. 8 in. |
| Hammer throw | 138 ft. |
| Shot-put | 47 ft. 9 in. |
| Javelin | 138 ft. |
| Discus | 125 ft. 8 in. |

## JIM THORPE'S RECORD IN
## MAJOR LEAGUE BASEBALL

### Batting Record

| Team | Year | Games | At Bat | Hits | Average |
|---|---|---|---|---|---|
| New York Giants | 1913 | 19 | 35 | 5 | .143 |
| New York Giants | 1914 | 30 | 31 | 6 | .193 |
| New York Giants | 1915 | 17 | 52 | 12 | .231 |
| Cincinnati Reds | 1917 | 77 | 251 | 62 | .247 |
| New York Giants | 1917 | 26 | 57 | 11 | .193 |
| New York Giants | 1918 | 58 | 113 | 28 | .248 |
| New York Giants | 1919 | 2 | 3 | 1 | .333 |
| Boston Braves | 1919 | 60 | 156 | 51 | .327 |

## Fielding Record

| Team | Year | Games | z<br>Position | Fielding<br>Average |
|------|------|-------|----------|---------|
| New York | 1913 | 6 | Outfield | .994 |
| New York | 1914 | 4 | Outfield | .750 |
| New York | 1915 | 15 | Outfield | .933 |
| Cincinnati | 1917 | 71 | Outfield | .959 |
| New York | 1917 | 20 | Outfield | .969 |
| New York | 1918 | 44 | Outfield | .983 |
| New York | 1919 | 2 | Outfield | 1.000 |
| Boston | 1919 | 41 | Outfield | .926 |
| Boston | 1919 | 2 | 1st base | .867 |

## JIM THORPE'S FOOTBALL RECORD

1908—Walter Camp All-American—Third team halfback

1911—Walter Camp All-American—First team halfback

1912—Walter Camp All-American—First team halfback

Long Runs—60 yards, 75 yards, 85 yards for touchdowns against Pennsylvania

53 yards, 45 yards for touchdowns against Pittsburgh

50 yards twice for touchdowns against Brown

70 and 120 yards for touchdowns against Lafayette

40 yards for touchdown against Georgetown

In the Harvard-Carlisle game in 1912, Thorpe gained 173 of the 334 yards gained by the Indian team, all through rushing

In the Pittsburgh game, Thorpe scored 28 of his team's total of 34; against Army 22 of his team's 27. Against Harvard, Thorpe scored all the Indians' 18 points to defeat Percy Haughton's squad, 18-15

Against Army, he ran almost 200 yards (because of an offside) to score a touchdown

Field Goals—Against Harvard, 1911, 4 field goals, one from just inside the 50-yard stripe

Conversions—Against Pittsburgh, 6 in one game, 1912

Kicking—70 yards against Pittsburgh

Better than 70 yards against Lafayette

Iigh Scoring—198 points in 1912 (never equaled by a major school)

920—Elected president of the American Professional Football Association

1950—Voted greatest football player of the first half of the twentieth century (Associated Press Poll of Sports Writers and broadcasters throughout the country)

## JIM THORPE'S OLYMPIC RECORDS—1912
### Pentathlon

200-meter race—1st place ............................................ 22.9 seconds
1500-meter race—1st place ................. 4 minutes 40.8 seconds
Broad jump—1st place ...................................23 ft. 2-7/10 in.
Discus—1st place ............................................. 116 ft. 8-4/10 in.
Javelin—3rd place .......................................... 153 ft. 2-19/20 in.

### Decathlon

1500 meter race—1st place ................. 4 minutes 40.1 seconds
110 meter high hurdles—1st place ....................... 15.6 seconds
High jump—1st place ................................... 6 ft. 1-6/10 in.
Shot-put—1st place ................................... 42 ft. 5-9/20 in.
Broad jump—3rd place ............................... 22 ft. 2-3/10 in.
Pole vault—3rd place ..................................... 10 ft. 7-19/20 in.
Discus—3rd place ...................................... 121 ft. 3-9/10 in.
100-meter race—3rd place ............................... 11.2 seconds
400-meter race—4th place ................................ 52.2 seconds
Javelin—4th place ...................................... 149 ft. 11-2/10 in.

Jim Thorpe won the Pentathlon with the low score of 7 points

Jim Thorpe won the Decathlon with 8,412.96 points

# INDEX

## About the Author

GENE SCHOOR was born in Passaic, New Jersey, and graduated from high school a four-letter man in football, baseball, basketball and boxing. He was mostly interested in boxing and won fifty-two out of fifty-five bouts during his collegiate career at the University of Miami. After graduation, he was boxing coach at the University of Minnesota, and then came to New York City where he taught boxing and Health Education at CCNY and NYU. He has done newspaper and radio work, has produced sport shows with such famous people as Joe DiMaggio, Jack Dempsey, Phil Rizzuto, and has written many biographies on sport personalities.